The Nonprofit Handbook: Management

Third Edition

2002 Supplement

WILEY NONPROFIT LAW, FINANCE, AND MANAGEMENT SERIES

The Nonprofit Handbook: Management

Third Edition

2002 Supplement

**Edited by
Tracy Daniel Connors**

John Wiley & Sons, Inc.

Copyright © 2002 by John Wiley & Sons, Inc., New York.

Library of Congress Cataloging in Publication Data:
The nonprofit handbook. Management/edited by Tracy Daniel Connors.—3rd ed.
    p. cm.—(Wiley nonprofit law, finance, and management series)
    Includes bibliographical references and index.
    ISBN 0-471-39799-7 (cloth: alk. paper), 0-471-419389 (supplement)
    1. Nonprofit organizations—Management—Handbooks, manuals, etc. 2. Nonprofit organizations—Finance—Handbooks, manuals, etc. 3. Total quality management—Handbooks, manuals, etc. I. Title: Management. II. Connors, Tracy Daniel. III. Series.

HD62.6.N662 2001
658'.048—dc21   00-061960

Printed in the United States of America

10 9 8 7 6 5 4 3 2 1

Update Service

BECOME A SUBSCRIBER!

Did you purchase this product from a bookstore?

If you did, it's important for you to become a subscriber. John Wiley & Sons, Inc. may publish, on a periodic basis, supplements and new editions to reflect the latest changes in the subject matter that you *need to know* in order to stay competitive in this ever-changing industry. By contacting the Wiley office nearest you, you'll receive any current update at no additional charge. In addition, you'll receive future updates and revised or related volumes on a 30-day examination review.

If you purchased this product directly from John Wiley & Sons, Inc., we have already recorded your subscription for this update service.

To become a subscriber, please call **1-800-225-5945** or send your name, company name (if applicable), address, and the title of the product to:

mailing address: **Supplement Department**
                          John Wiley & Sons, Inc.
                          One Wiley Drive
                          Somerset, NJ 08875

e-mail: **subscriber@wiley.com**
fax: **1-732-302-2300**
online: **www.wiley.com**

For customers outside the United States, please contact the Wiley office nearest you:

Professional & Reference Division
John Wiley & Sons Canada, Ltd.
22 Worcester Road
Rexdale, Ontario M9W 1L1
CANADA
(416) 675-3580
Phone: 1-800-567-4797
Fax: 1-800-565-6802
canada@wiley.com

John Wiley & Sons, Ltd.
Baffins Lane
Chichester
West Sussex, PO19 1UD
ENGLAND
Phone: (44) 1243 779777
Fax: (44) 1243 770638
cs-books@wiley.co.uk

Jacaranda Wiley Ltd.
PRT Division
P.O. Box 174
North Ryde, NSW 2113
AUSTRALIA
Phone: (02) 805-1100
Fax: (02) 805-1597
headoffice@jacwiley.com.au

John Wiley & Sons (SEA) Pte. Ltd.
37 Jalan Pemimpin
Block B # 05-04
Union Industrial Building
SINGAPORE 2057
Phone: (65) 258-1157
Fax: (65) 463-4604
enquiry@wiley.com.sg

About the Editor

For twenty-five years, **Tracy Daniel Connors** has served as executive editor for numerous best-selling, comprehensive handbooks for leaders and managers of nonprofit organizations. In addition, he has served in a variety of management positions in business, government, and philanthropy. Captain Connors retired from the U.S. Navy in 1999. Voluntarily recalled as a Naval Reservist to active duty frequently since 1985, most recently he served on the staff of the Secretary of the Navy as Director of Systems Integration/Quality of Life Broadcast Network for LIFE-Lines; as director of Congressional & Public Affairs for the Space and Naval Warfare Systems Command and the Naval Sea Systems Command in Washington, DC; as Deputy Director of the Navy's Command Excellence and Leader Development Program; and as the first Total Quality Leadership Public Affairs Officer for the Chief of Naval Operations. Other private and public sector positions have included Director of Satellite Learning Services for the U.S. Chamber of Commerce; chief of staff for a senior member of Congress; corporate communication manager for a major electronics corporation; vice president of a national publishing corporation; and as an officer, board member, or professional staff director of numerous not-for-profit organizations. He attended Jacksonville University, graduated from the University of Florida, and earned a Master of Arts degree from the University of Rhode Island. He served as Executive Editor for the *Nonprofit Organization Handbook* (McGraw-Hill, 1979–1989), the first comprehensive management handbook for nonprofit organizations. The *Nonprofit Handbook: Management*, Third Edition (John Wiley & Sons, 2001), for which he serves as Executive Editor, is the first Wiley management handbook for nonprofit organizations to be published in a third edition. He is also the editor of the *Volunteer Management Handbook;* the *Nonprofit Management Handbook, Operating Policies & Procedures; Financial Management for Nonprofit Organizations; The Dictionary of Mass Media and Communication;* and *Flavors of the Fjords: The Norwegian Holiday Cookbook.* Currently, he is completing a new work focusing on fighter-bomber operations during the Korean War.

Contributors

Sylvia Allen, MA, is president of Allen Consulting, Inc., a nationally known sports and events marketing company located in New Jersey. She is a published author, publisher of *The Sponsorship Newsletter,* and teaches sponsorship and sports marketing at New York University and at roughly one hundred conferences annually.

Joseph E. Champoux, PhD, is professor of management at the Robert O. Anderson Schools of Management at the University of New Mexico. His research activities have included total quality management, the organization and management effects of modern manufacturing, job design, and the relationship between work and nonwork. His current research activities focus on film as a teaching resource.

Dan R. Dyble, MSOD, is an associate of the WELLTH Learning Network and The International Institute for Cultural Transition. He has worked with both for-profit and nonprofit organizations across Canada and the United States. Coming from an operations background, he has held management positions in several industries. His research has focused on conflict across cultures. His passions revolve around practices that grow and evolve organizations and their clarity.

Stephen Hobbs, EdD, is the creator of the WELLTH Learning Network and co-founder of The International Institute for Cultural Transition. His work experience lists manager in nonprofit and public organizations as well as corporate trainer and facilitator. He has consulted and presented in Canada, the United States, Australia, and Eastern Africa. His practice focuses on culture and transition; workplace learning at the personal, team, and organizational levels; and manager as educator. Also, he shares what he learns with adult learners involved in the Certificate in Adult Learning, University of Calgary.

Donna Kennedy-Glans, BA, LLB, is an international energy expert with more than 15 years of experience managing private-sector interests in international projects in the developing world. Ms. Kennedy-Glans has focused on nontechnical risk evaluation and management in challenging jurisdictions. Her expertise in risk management is built on solid international legal, commercial, and operational experience within a framework of respect for corporate social accountability. Ms. Kennedy-Glans has also applied her expertise to the support of humanitarian initiatives by Canadian nonprofit organizations in the developing world.

Ms. Kennedy-Glans is the President of The Kennedy-Glans Perspective Inc., a consulting company that advises private, public, and nonprofit organizations on management of nontechnical risks in international jurisdictions.

Richard L. Thompson, APR, MS (Marketing), is Director of Communications and Public Affairs at the Naval Research Laboratory, Washington, DC. His 29 years of marketing communications practice have focused in the areas of business-to-

business, business-to-government, and government-to-government high-technology marketing communications and public relations program management, specializing in contingency and special event planning for the for-profit, nonprofit, and government business sectors. Mr. Thompson, a Public Relations Society of America accredited practitioner, has planned and conducted contingency and emergency communications operations for high-technology, defense, and military clients throughout the United States and overseas.

▼ Preface

In this the first supplement to the *Nonprofit Handbook: Management,* Third Edition, we have provided what we believe are the best of the proven approaches to the more effective operation and management of nonprofit organizations, in an accessible, readily useable format. In addition, through the inherent flexibility of the supplementation system, we provide information and guidance in new or rapidly developing areas of nonprofit policy and management.

In these annual supplements, as in the *Handbook,* we review and outline the policies and practices operating and evolving in the major areas of nonprofit management that improve effectiveness, efficiency, and leadership. In addition, we try to provide useful combinations of tips and checklists, further complemented by real-world examples and illustrations.

Chapters added to this supplement since publication of the bound edition have enabled us to expand our coverage of management areas important to the success of nonprofit organization leaders. We are particularly pleased to add to this series new contributors whose impressive expertise provides important additional coverage in such areas as marketing and communications, information management, resource development, organization environment, and human resource development.

We welcome Richard Thompson, Stephen Hobbs, Dan Dyble, Sylvia Allen, Dr. Joseph Champoux, and Donna Kennedy-Glans to this supplement. Their chapters provide important new solutions for nonprofit leaders faced with the challenges of competition and regulation. In addition, they provide timely information on how to effectively use the many new resources and tools that offer great potential for nonprofit organizations.

The tragic events of September 11, 2001 reinforced and underscored the importance of effective management and visionary leadership for nonprofit organizations around the world. Richard Thompson, APR, reviewed, revised and enlarged his timely, highly useful "Contingency and Emergency Public Affairs" chapter and incorporated new emphasis on crisis communications and management strategies and planning. He has provided important insights into how nonprofit leaders and managers can anticipate and cope with public affairs contingencies and emergencies ranging from "worst case" disasters to the "routine" disruptions of operations, such as computer failure or hacking.

Dr. Stephen Hobbs and Dan Dyble of the WELLTH Learning Network focus on management evaluation of data, particularly for volunteer resource managers in their ground breaking chapter, "Making Your Data Collection Meaningful." Within the nonprofit, voluntary action sector, the shift to using business acumen— "social entrepreneurship"—continues to gain momentum. By using business tools and techniques, social entrepreneurs are developing and introducing new solutions to community concerns and issues. Using scare resources more effectively is essential to successful program management. Data management, in turn, is the indispensable component of any sustainable program. Hobbs and Dyble explain and outline the key issues in meaningful data collection, then provide key insights into managing a volunteer resource management system, including data collection assessment, evaluation, and how to manage "the answers from the questions."

While it is no secret that it is increasingly difficult for nonprofits to raise money due to growing competition for the same dollars, knowing how and when to approach individuals and organizations does offer an "edge" over those who continue to "follow the traditional paths," explains Sylvia Allen in "Sales for Nonprofits." Knowing the difference between Sponsorship and Fundraising, identifying useful information contained in annual reports, uncovering the secrets of cause-related marketing, understanding corporate marketing and philanthropy, following the rules for success and profiling the characteristics of effective salespeople are explained and developed by Ms. Allen, a highly successful consultant and practitioner in her own right.

Organizational culture includes its history, values, norms, rites, rituals, ceremonies, heroes and scoundrels—all of which strongly influence and affect its members and constituency. In "Organizational Culture and Nonprofit Organizations," Dr. Joseph E. Champoux explains the levels of organizational culture, its symbolism and functions, the dysfunctions of organizational culture and their diagnosis, and how to create and institutionalize a new organizational culture "that sustains changes in an organization over time."

In the increasingly interconnected world in which we live and function, markets, nations and technologies are integrated to a degree almost unimaginable just a short time ago. Ever improving communications technologies have expanded by orders of magnitude the exchange of ideas, information and strategies between regional, national, hemispheric and global volunteer organizations. Voluntary organizations are increasingly responding to complex global challenges and opportunities. How the organization manages its risks and challenges in the highly variable international setting is the subject of Donna Kennedy-Glans' chapter entitled, "Volunteer Organization Management Processes and Challenges in the International Context." After outlining a framework for analysis of management processes that minimize risk in international operations, Ms. Kennedy-Glans highlights and explains those processes that identify and manage inherent risks in the international context.

The selection of these subjects and contributors reflects your input and recommendations. You told us through your letters and feedback that you needed additional coverage of these topics. Why not let us hear from you regarding the *Handbook* and its supplements? We review carefully every letter, comment, and recommendation. Your communications help us constantly improve our service to you. We welcome your recommendations for subjects, coverage, case studies, examples, and illustrations. We would also like to hear from you regarding future contributors, including yourself if you believe you have the requisite background and experience.

Finally, we would like to say thanks to all of you who have become part of the *Nonprofit Handbook* "family." Speaking for all the contributors, we deeply appreciate your support and encouragement.

Tracy Daniel Connors
Fogland Point, Tiverton, Rhode Island

SUPPLEMENT CONTENTS

Note to the Reader: Sections not in the main bound volumes are indicated by "(New)" after the title. Material from the main volume that has been updated for this supplement is indicated by "(Revised)" after the title.

Effectiveness

MARKETING & COMMUNICATIONS

INFORMATION MANAGEMENT

13 Contingency and Emergency Public Affairs (Revised)

RICHARD L. THOMPSON, APR, MS, DIRECTOR OF
COMMUNICATIONS AND PUBLIC AFFAIRS
Naval Research Laboratory, Washington, DC

13.1 Introduction

Following the events of September 11, nonprofit communications practitioners and their management teams need to rethink how crisis communications and management should be conducted. While most nonprofits have baseline crisis and contingency public affairs plans, many are outdated, too media or customer driven, or too simplistic or complex to be executed. With the nation engaged in a long-term war on terrorism at home and abroad with the possibility of additional terrorist acts, public affairs professionals should review their contingency and disaster plans and candidly assess their ability to respond. This includes a catastrophic situation that virtually shuts down the organization's ability to operate.

While planning for the worst case is important, public affairs contingencies and emergencies must also plan for less severe disruptions of routine operations, such as computer failure involving breakdowns or hacking, or an accident involving injury or death. They may also include other occurrences that reflect badly on the organization, such as employee drug abuse incident, fraud, mismanagement, improper hazardous waste disposal, and the like. The bottom line is that a public affairs contingency or emergency situation can be a real or perceived threat that has the potential to disrupt normal operations, prevents the nonprofit organization from attaining its goals, or could cause an adverse reaction among stakeholders.

Regardless of the nature of operations, proper response to a contingency or emergency demands careful preplanning, constant testing and evaluation, mature judgment, and appropriate action taken without hesitation throughout the organization. One vital component of a nonprofit organization's response in a contingency or emergency is communication with concerned stakeholders.

The purpose of this chapter is to provide basic guidance to assist organization leaders, managers, and their public affairs executives in meeting their public affairs responsibilities in a wide variety of contingencies—incidents, accidents, and other emergencies.

13.2   Public Affairs Practitioner and Staff

During a contingency or emergency, the public affairs practitioner and staff are key elements of the management team providing direct support to the organization leadership. In the event of a crisis, the public affairs staff should employ a variety of internal information systems—e-mail, faxes, bulletins, Intranet/Internet Web pages, newsletters—to keep staff and stakeholders informed as crisis response proceeds. In a public information capacity, the public affairs staff informs both the internal and external stakeholders of the incident and the organization's actions to control it.

13.3   Public Affairs Contingency Plan

The most effective way to deal with and respond to a contingency or emergency is to have a public affairs plan in place before anything happens. This plan should—at a minimum—provide the methodology, processes, logistics, and training doctrine to:

- Provide relief and recovery from the contingency or emergency
- Reduce exposure and manage the risk to the organization
- Protect the organization's credibility and image with stakeholders, including the general public

This plan should anticipate and prepare for a wide range of contingencies, up to and including destruction of the organization's facility and the loss of key management members. Your plan should incorporate communications plans to notify the organization structure (both up and down), local support agencies, customers, stockholders, clients, members, and others in the event of any accident, incident, or contingency.

Employees, clients, customers, members, and the public have a legitimate interest in an occurrence that adversely impacts your organization or operations, leading to injury, death, or extensive damage to property. To plan for and to be responsive and forthcoming in such situations:

- The public affairs director should be a participating member of panels, boards, or teams concerned with the planning for and response to crises and emergencies.

- Public affairs should be an element for consideration in all contingency and emergency planning.
- Public affairs actions should be prescribed in all organization contingency or emergency action plans.
- The senior leadership should promptly notify the public affairs director or designated alternate when any incident, occurrence, or situation develops that has potential for causing reaction on the part of the news media or the general public.
- The organization's senior public affairs practitioners should be contacted for advice and counsel in an emergency or for contingency planning.

Contingency and emergency planning, like public affairs, is a management function that is coordinated and done in conjunction with other departments within the organization. Organizations should plan for contingencies and emergencies the same way they operate on a daily basis—as a team.

The contingency planning team should include senior members from management, legal, public affairs, operations/customer service, security, finance/supply, management information/computer operations, human resources, facilities management, administrative services, in-house and contractor technical experts, and other stakeholders, depending on your organization. Cross-training of team members is critical and expertise in more than one area can be crucial in the event that not all crisis management team members are available. Identifying the most appropriate and skilled members for your crisis team is not an easy task. Often, the best team members are not the people with the highest-ranking titles, but those who possess the required skills, talents, and personality to handle each function of crisis management. Carefully screening and selecting individuals who are right for contingency and emergency operation is one of the most critical decisions you can make.

When you pick your team, let your players know. Team members who have a role to play are more likely to prepare for a crisis and take the time to think through potential responses. Depending on the type and magnitude of your crisis, you may need to mobilize your entire team, or just a few select members. So be sure you have established a foolproof method of notifying team members for quick response.

Planning for contingencies and emergencies is more than just preparing a written plan. Planning is a process, not a product. Contingency and emergency planning is a dynamic process that must be molded to the organization's changing internal and external environment. Effective contingency and emergency planning requires an active planning and training senior management team. In preparing the public affairs contingency plan, it is useful to have and follow a checklist. The following public affairs contingency checklist can be used as a guideline for planning purposes:

- Who is the first public affairs official to be notified?
- Who is notified if that person is not available?
- Who is responsible for notifying the public affairs person?
- Who of the public affairs staff is to be notified and mobilized? How will that notification be achieved?

- Who notifies the public affairs staff?
- Who is the organization's primary media spokesperson? What training and background do they have in contingency/crisis public affairs?
- Who is the alternate spokesperson?
- Who notifies the media?
- What is the process by which news and information are processed and approved for release?
- Who notifies employees?
- Where is the pressroom? Where is the briefing room?
- Who will be the secretary in the pressroom?
- Who will be the messenger in the pressroom?
- Who will gather factual information and relay it to the pressroom?
- Who will arrange for food and supplies in the pressroom?
- Who will arrange for transportation from the pressroom to the site, if not collocated?
- Who will transport the press from the pressroom to the site?
- Who in the organization will review and approve information before it is released to the press?
- What is the senior management team interface process for approval of public affairs policy and release clearance?
- What statements, if any, will be released by the organization?
- How will press inquiries to the organization be handled and processed?
- Who decides if media can visit the site?
- Who will accompany the media on site visits?
- Who are the public information officers for area organizations, city, county, state, and so on? How will they be informed?
- How will your organization coordinate public information operations with other organizations?
- Who can take photos/video for your organization?
- Who will maintain a record of press contacts and monitor press coverage?
- Who will correct the record should incorrect information be communicated by the media?

Keep a folder with incident/accident instructions, local and organization public affairs telephone numbers, and a list of established local organizational public affairs procedures. Include instruction pages from various organization manuals and current policy references that deal with contingencies.

In addition, preformatted contingency press releases that allow the user to either fill in the blanks or mix and match should be included. Update this material periodically. Ensure that the contingency and emergency plans are easily understood so that someone outside the public affairs staff can initiate the plan in the event you are not available. Make certain that each member of the organization's crisis response team has this plan on the office computer, a laptop, or on disk at home, and a hard copy.

13.4 Public Affairs Goals during a Contingency or Emergency

Detailed instructions cannot be provided to cover every possible contingency; however, certain general actions are appropriate in most circumstances. Public affairs goals in a contingency or emergency include the following:

- Safeguarding people and protecting property
- Ensuring that civil authorities are provided prompt and correct information to enable them to make decisions concerning protection of the public
- Retaining public confidence in the organization
- Respecting the rights of organization personnel to privacy and protecting their welfare and the dignity of the next-of-kin
- Honoring the right of the public to be informed rapidly and accurately of accidents and incidents and the organization's response in emergencies and other contingencies

It is during a time of crisis that your knowledge of the local media is most valuable. Relations with members of the general media in your area, and specific trade media in your business sector, should be constant and ongoing. An organization's working relationships with local media—that is, the ability to contact a media representative who is familiar with your organization—gives a public affairs practitioner a significant head start in solving a contingency or emergency communications situation.

(A) RELEASE OF INFORMATION

Accurate public affairs assessments are essential elements of an organization's evaluation of and report on a crisis or emergency. Public affairs assessments must be included in incident reports to higher levels of authority within your organization. The rapid release of accurate, factual information concerning an accident, incident, disaster, or other emergency is in the best interest of an organization.

Speed and accuracy are vital. However, a release containing incorrect or speculative information may create panic and confusion. Conversely, an accurate release that is too late to inform the public is of little or no value. Although most details are unavailable and a comprehensive picture is elusive in the early stages of a contingency, rapid initial release of known, confirmed facts provides valuable information to the community.

When passed to higher elements of your organization, the initial release also alerts a larger public affairs network to render assistance to the local organization involved. If media representatives are at your location or nearby at the time of the accident, full cooperation should be rendered in covering the story, consistent with safety, protection of property and information at the site, and other pertinent requirements. Organizations should modify or expand the following public affairs assessments as required to fit their local situation:

- No media present
- Media present, press release follows
- No media present, media interest expected
- No known press interest
- Public concern anticipated; proposed statement and contingency questions and answers to follow
- Local media on scene, the following statement was made at (date/time): [summary of statement]

When an accident or significant incident occurs, the public affairs practitioner must be notified immediately. Depending on the situation, the public affairs practitioner must have the authority to recall some or all of the staff, and prepare, properly staff, and disseminate information to the news media. The organization should draft the initial release and forward it to higher authority for release or release it locally; the information is not held pending inquiry. The goal for initial release should be one hour from the time the public affairs office is first notified of the occurrence and the time information is prepared for initial release. Within the next hour, the majority of local and other interested news media are informed. This is a goal, although situational constraints may cause initial release to take longer. Be right the first time.

During a crisis situation, it is especially important that the organization have only one spokesperson. Establish who that person is in advance; designate an alternate. If too many individuals talk to the media, conflicting or out-of-date information will be presented, resulting in an impression that information management by the organization is poor and, ultimately, not credible. (This impression will have a longer-term impact on overall public support—including funding—on which nonprofits depend.) Strongly suggest to the media that if they haven't heard it from the designated spokesperson, they haven't heard it correctly. Then "turn off" the unauthorized spokesperson.

The organization spokesperson is the final point of quality control prior to release of information. The spokesperson must ensure that the following six elements are considered and achieved prior to release:

1. *Gather and relate accurate information.* Consider how the public affairs organization will discover the facts, keep management informed, notify next-of-kin (if a fatality or serious injury is involved), and deal with media.
2. *Consider legal aspects carefully.* Consider how the organization will determine or be affected by legal liabilities, possible violations, and so on, and delegate this responsibility to a qualified legal counsel early in the public affairs contingency process.
3. *Provide full, factual, objective, truthful information.* Resist inclinations—your own or others'—to slant, distort, manipulate, or fragment the truth. Being discovered in a lie will be much more damaging than anything an unfavorable truth might cause.
4. *Gather, verify, and complete all units of information before release to the media.* Avoid giving out partial, unchecked facts that could result in repeated

media mention with undue emphasis on bad news. Avoid the appearance of noncooperation.

5. *Ensure accuracy, thoroughness, and completeness by providing information packages and Web sites.* Press conferences, information sheets, handouts, prepared statements for broadcast appearances, e-mails, Web pages, and (in the final stages) press kits will contribute to effective communication when an emergency requires disseminating information to the media simultaneously.

6. *Emphasize perspective by balancing bad news with good.* The organization's reputation, earned over the years, should not be forgotten in a crisis.

(B) DENIAL AND ADVERSE INFORMATION

One way to create a public affairs problem for an organization is to deny that a particular event occurred when it did. If an organization has a contingency or emergency situation, either release the information or respond to media query with approved responses. The goal is to keep a one-day news story as just that: a one-day story. Denial or "no comment" on a bad news story will only prolong the issue and reinforce negative impressions among your public on whom you depend for support, funding, and volunteers.

(C) NEWS RELEASES

Do not eliminate adverse information from a story. Present the facts without opinion and in detail. Your incident/accident story will then be given the treatment it deserves. If you create a situation in which reporters are forced to guess, or even more dangerous, seek out "a source" (an informer), you can expect inquiries from every level within your organization into the incident, including the information release policies of your office.

The initial release should provide as much information as possible on the key points. It is extremely important that information be released to the public as soon as possible; the rapid release of information prevents or dispels rumors that could easily cause public alarm or promote misinformation in news media reports. Newly arriving media representatives can be updated later.

In general, initial and follow-on releases should include the following:

- Type of incident, accident, or contingency
- Location and time of the incident, accident, or contingency
- Persons involved. Initially, release number injured and killed, if known. Also, the number of staff and volunteers. Don't speculate—if you don't know, say so. Then find out as soon as possible.
- If a transportation-related incident or accident, the place of departure and destination. This pertains to vehicles, aircraft, vessels, and the like.
- Type of equipment or system involved
- Pertinent facts about activities or operations at the time of the incident or accident
- Investigation. Never speculate about the cause or contributing causes of an accident or the responsibility for the mishap. If the situation warrants,

ensure that you release information stating that an investigation into the cause is being conducted by the proper authorities and that corrective measures are being taken. For example, if there is an environmental waste disposal problem, you should be prepared to tell the public what your organization is doing to clean it up and to prevent future occurrences.

(D) RELEASE OF INFORMATION PERTAINING TO EMPLOYEES OR VOLUNTEERS

Whenever possible, the public affairs practitioner must coordinate with the human resources office or other designated organization department prior to releasing information on employees who have been injured or killed in accidents. There are several critical aspects in releasing information pertaining to employees or volunteers involved in accidents:

- Information must not be released to news media until confirmation is received that next-of-kin have been notified. Thereafter, information released to media must agree with that provided to the next-of-kin. This means that the next-of-kin are advised of details before the media are, and that the media are not given any information that is not provided to the next-of-kin.
- Following medical care for the injured, the rights and dignity of the persons involved in accidents and their next-of-kin are of paramount importance. However, the public's right to know takes on new importance in regard to accidents, incidents, and other disasters. Releasing the names of accident victims can relieve the anxiety and concern of relatives and friends of those not injured. Early and ongoing liaison with the human resources office point-of-contact will enable the organization to release names as soon as possible after the accident.
- Should an accident occur off the organization's property, but employees are involved, news media on the scene may be able to obtain identification without consulting the public affairs practitioner. Humanitarian considerations dictate that the next-of-kin be notified of the situation before they learn of it through the news media. If it is apparent that news media know the identity of accident victims and next-of-kin have not been notified, the public affairs practitioner should make a professional appeal to the reporters or editors requesting that they withhold names of persons involved until notification is made. It is critical to inform the human resources office of the results of this appeal and the personnel whose names are likely to be known by the reporters. Knowing and having an established relationship with local and regional editors prior to the occurrence can make the critical difference between success and failure in this area.

(E) HELPING FAMILY MEMBERS DEAL WITH THE PRESS

During times of crisis, your organization's employees, volunteers, and families may become the targets of news media attention as reporters try to localize or give an emotional edge to the story. It is easy to blame the press for a lack of compassion, but the truth is that many families don't realize that once they are publicly identified, they become targets for other reporters and the general public.

Some important things family members should know about dealing with the press include the following:

- News is an extremely competitive business, with reporters going to great lengths to "get the story" before their competitors.
- It is the right of the individual to say no to an interview request. In the past, some reporters have coerced family members into submitting to interviews by emphasizing the public's right to know and freedom of the press, but your right to privacy always takes precedence.
- The individual's home is private property; no one, media or otherwise, has a right to enter your home, or be on your property, unless you grant them that privilege.
- If the subject under scrutiny does decide to talk with the media, ground rules for that protection should be established before the interview. Responsible professional reporters will work to meet reasonable ground rules. These ground rules are often negotiated or brokered by the public affairs practitioner, who represents and provides counsel to the interviewee. The public affairs practitioner will discuss and seek agreement of the ground rules with the media representative prior to any direct contact with the interviewee. Ground rules can include no photos/video of faces, disguising of voices, nonattribution of comments, and the like.
- Family members may not wish to have their full names used, and you should always ensure that the home address is not used. Television pictures of an employee or volunteer's house are usually not a good idea.

13.5 Incidents or Accidents outside Your Facility

Should an incident or accident occur outside your facility, the public affairs challenge becomes more complex. From a logistics standpoint, the public affairs team must then operate from two locations, the public affairs office and the accident site, with public affairs representatives at both locations. This complicates communications, transportation, and public information clearance procedures. This eventuality should be anticipated and addressed in your planning.

Consistent with organizational, legal, and operational constraints, your organization should give maximum cooperation to news representatives covering incidents and accidents. Immediately following an accident or incident, the organization should:

- Take action to minimize further injury and property damage
- Assist in rescue of survivors and treatment of the injured
- Report the incident or accident to the proper authority
- Preserve the accident scene to assist investigators

- Protect organization files and records
- Consult with civil authorities if activating public warning or evacuation plans may be appropriate
- Rapidly meet the need for public information about the accident or incident

No two contingencies are identical, but public affairs actions at an off-site location should include the following:

- *Defining the area.* Upon arrival at the accident scene, the senior public affairs official should request that law enforcement or public safety authorities rope off the entire area to protect the public from injury and property from further disturbance.
- *Briefing the reporters.* The organization should prepare contingency questions and answers to respond to likely news media inquiries at the incident or accident scene. Once statements or contingency answers are approved, the senior public affairs official at the scene should be granted permission to release the preapproved information. In addition, reporters should be briefed on safety hazards (if any) and the need to preserve the site for investigators before they are permitted to enter the cordoned-off area. The briefing should be done by the public affairs official at the scene who can get information from others present. If a reporter refuses to cooperate with the ground rules, you have the option to request that security personnel deny access to the individual. Keep in mind that you may not physically restrict the movement of the news media at accident sites, except on your property.
- *Admitting reporters to the area.* After the area is cordoned off, news media representatives are briefed, and law enforcement, public safety, and organization officials advise that an area is safe, the senior public affairs official on the scene may grant permission to enter the accident area.
- *Media identification.* As part of the public affairs office contingency planning, special news media identification badges may be required and should be kept on hand. These may consist of inexpensive plastic badges, arm bands, or other similar devices that conform to the organization's security badging system and are ready for immediate issue in the event of an incident or other emergency. Badges can be prepared in advance, with one or more badges marked and set aside for each local newspaper, several for each television station, and so on. The badges can be taken to the accident scene by the public affairs office member assigned that duty by the organization's contingency planning. Wearing the badge signifies to the organization and law enforcement personnel that the wearer has been briefed on safety considerations regarding the accident site and the need to preserve the site for investigators. More importantly, the badge system can ease confusion at a busy, crowded site. Reporters' wearing of such identification is voluntary in areas outside your property, but can be required of them when at your facility.

As soon as possible following the conclusion of the event, the public affairs practitioner should develop a narrative summary of public affairs actions taken before and following the contingency, as a training tool to critique the staff and share lessons learned. The summary should be shared with the rest of the organization. A cassette tape recorder is quite helpful for making notes during fast-moving situations.

13.6 Contingency Public Affairs Do's and Don'ts

Do's

- Get the facts before you talk with the press.
- Establish who is going to speak for the organization.
- Get information to the press as quickly as possible and be aware of press deadlines.
- Issue statements in writing if at all possible.
- Emphasize the positive.
- Know to whom you are speaking. Get the reporter's name and get the name and telephone number in telephone interviews. Log all media queries on media query forms.
- Aid media representatives in getting the story.
- Monitor media coverage, including the Internet, and correct errors quickly.
- Say "I don't know" if you don't know. Follow up by taking the question and state that you will try to get the answer.

Don'ts

- Don't say "No comment."
- Don't guess or speculate—ever!
- Don't release damage estimates without double-checking for accuracy.
- Don't release names of victims until notification of next-of-kin has been made. Then confirm again that notification has been made.
- Don't try to mislead or cover up information. Never lie.
- Don't try to place blame.
- Don't play favorites with the media. Release information to everyone at the same time.
- Don't ever make off-the-record comments. There is no such thing.
- Don't use inflammatory, spectacular terms like *blown to bits, raging fire,* or *torn limb from limb.*
- Don't repeat negative or inaccurate statements in answering questions.
- Don't panic, cry, or lose control.

13.7 Who Has Release Authority?

Who in your organization has the authority to release news? Important news releases are in effect announcements by the senior administrator concerning major appointments, policy, or matters of sufficient importance that justify release from the highest level in the organization. This also includes news that may affect organization policy or have a political impact.

Information that affects the entire organization may be released by the organization headquarters. The news release and information could be researched and developed by your department or division and provided to the organization headquarters for further staffing and approval prior to release. Depending on the size of the organization, there may be several levels of hierarchy to negotiate prior to reaching headquarters.

Matters concerning an individual organization, such as announcements of limited interest (local achievements, background materials, etc.) may be released at the local level. If you have any doubt about your authority in a given situation, you should contact public affairs officials at a more senior level of your organization before you talk to the press.

13.8   Key Concepts in Managing a Crisis

The public affairs professional faces unique challenges as counselor, spokesperson, agency liaison, rumor control, and leader during a crisis or contingency. In the November 2001 issue of *Public Relations Tactics*, Richard M. Bridges, APR, Arlington County, Virginia's Assistant County Manager for Public Affairs, listed several lessons learned from his involvement with the September 11th terrorist attack on the Pentagon. His lessons learned are valuable in meeting the challenges faced by the public affairs professional managing a crisis.

- The ability to work jointly with other organizations is critical when multiple agencies are involved. If possible, it is best to know public affairs counterparts and their capabilities prior to the actual contingency.
- In a crisis or contingency situation, the best spokespersons are those who have experienced the situation personally. It is incumbent on the public affairs professional to carefully select the spokesperson for poise and presence in front of the media, and to prebrief the individual on talking points and areas to avoid.
- No matter how much information or access is provided, the media is rarely satisfied and always want more.
- Try to anticipate media needs. While the media are busy filing for deadline, anticipate their needs for tomorrow.
- Anticipate the unexpected. Every crisis or contingency provides a number of unexpected or unpleasant surprises. Think unconventionally.
- If you have a staff, use it; if you don't, get help. In a large-scale or long-term contingency, the public affairs professional must fulfill many roles almost simultaneously. No single person can successfully fulfill all these roles; trust in and rely on your staff for support.
- The news cycle 24/7. So that media queries are processed in an efficient manner, ensure public affairs staffing provides 24-hour staffing, but only if necessary.

- It is critical for the public affairs team to share the workload and pace themselves throughout the crisis/contingency period. It is important to have a surge capability and a reserve should something else occur.
- Use the crisis/contingency as a learning and teaching opportunity for the team and the staff. Document what went right, what did not work, and areas where improvements can be made. These situations also provide a valuable, hands-on learning experience for all involved.

13.9   The Mobile Public Affairs Office

With the rapidly expanding capabilities of laptop computer technology, increased hard drive storage, high data rate internal modems, increasingly user-friendly software, and the Internet, the mobile laptop office has become a reality. With the advent of powerful laptop computers with large-capacity hard drives and high-speed modems, Ethernet, and wireless communications capabilities bundled with popular software packages, at ever-decreasing prices, these systems have become a business essential for the public affairs practitioner and nonprofit executives. When coupled with a cellular telephone with plug-in modem capability, a pager, and a wireless communications-capable handheld organizer such as a Palm Pilot VIIx, the nonprofit executive has the capability to set up a mobile office virtually anywhere.

The savvy executive, with some thought and preparation, can load software programs and data that allow the laptop computer to become a multipurpose mobile office capable of not only word processing, desktop publishing, Web page development, database management, and spreadsheet development, but also a powerful communications tool for faxing information to both individuals and groups, and for corresponding directly with stakeholders via e-mail and the Internet.

Due to the rapid evolution of computer technology, I will avoid addressing particular systems, except to say that both recent-technology Windows and Macintosh operating system laptops provide more computing power that the average nonprofit executive will ever use. The same can be said for fax/modem, Ethernet, wireless communications, and printer technologies.

In the selection of a computer, the same rule that applies to desktop computers applies to laptop computers. Though the circuits, central processing units, and hard drives may be the same from one model to the next, pay close attention to the human/machine interface and ergonomics when purchasing. Of particular importance is determining whether the laptop keyboard (often smaller in size than a desktop computer keyboard) and display are comfortable to you. The best way to determine if you and a laptop are a good ergonomic fit is to perform a number of functions on the keyboard while viewing the screen in varying light conditions. If either your hands or your eyes feel strained, then search for another laptop with a better fit.

Other laptop features to look for include random access memory (RAM) expandability, a built-in mouse, infrared communication/networking and file transfer capability, built-in video monitor capability that allows you to connect to an external color monitor, and built-in modem/Ethernet capability.

Once you find the computer that suits your specific needs, the next task is selecting software and loading data to make it useful. Regardless of the operating system you use (Windows or Macintosh), there are literally thousands of software products on the market to fill your hard drive. Because you are mobile, it is recommended that you use *industry standard* software for word processing, desktop publishing, database, spreadsheet software, and communications software (for fax/modem and online services). Word Perfect, Microsoft Office, Adobe PageMaker, Adobe Pagemill, and others are widely accepted and offer a high degree of cross-platform (Windows to Macintosh and vice versa) compatibility. A personal information manager (PIM) that incorporates a calendar, electronic Rolodex, and to-do list is also important. As an example, 3Com's Palm Pilot handheld organizers are bundled with the Palm Desktop organizer software for the personal computer that incorporates an electronic address book, calendar, to-do list, memo pad, and expense report. This PIM software can be synchronized and updated by pressing one button either by wire connection or infrared file transfer. Many handheld organizers are now available with direct Internet and e-mail connection and transmission capabilities.

What would a nonprofit public affairs practitioner require to operate from a remote site on short notice? From a public affairs standpoint, the well-equipped laptop should include some or all of the following information:

- Executive biographies, history, product, and organization fact sheets (word processing or desktop publishing software)
- Calendar (PIM software)
- Electronic Rolodex with e-mail addresses (PIM software)
- To-do list (PIM software)
- Organization decision makers and key staff members list with names, addresses, fax, telephone, and e-mail (PIM software)
- Public affairs contingency plan with *fill-in-the-blank* contingency press releases (word processing or desktop publishing software)
- Media list with name, address, telephone, and e-mail (PIM software or database software, tab-separated entry with ability to export to fax/modem transmission software, word processing mail merge for envelope labels, letters/memoranda/press releases, and e-mail)
- Organization membership list with name, address, telephone, and e-mail (PIM software or database software, tab-separated entry with ability to export to fax/modem transmission software, word processing mail merge for envelope labels, letters/memoranda/press releases, and e-mail)
- Organization budget and obligations to date in the event you must operate away from your normal office (spreadsheet software)
- An inventory of supplies required to equip an off-site or remote office (database or spreadsheet software)

Other required equipment includes:

- Backup operating system and software program CDs/diskettes
- Backup CDs/diskettes of program data
- Serial, parallel port printer cables
- Electrical extension cord (batteries don't last forever)
- Spare, charged batteries
- RJ-11 duplex adapter (allows you to plug a phone and a modem into a single wall telephone jack)

- 25 feet of telephone wire
- Ethernet cable for network connections
- Blank diskettes

While operating away from your office, there are normally three options in terms of printing:

1. Use of a printer on-site
2. Carrying a laptop portable printer
3. Use of a local fax machine as a printer

Unless you are planning to be off-site for an extended period, seriously consider options 1 and 3. Borrowing an on-site laser printer when away from your office is a good option, and use of a plain paper laser fax provides high-quality printing. Consider these options before carrying a three- to four-pound portable printer that often provides less quality or speed.

Communicating via fax/modem is now much easier, because many office, hotel, and pay telephones are equipped with data ports. Using a fax/modem allows you to transmit and receive your e-mail messages from your online service mailbox, or to transmit a fax. Emerging wireless communications technology also offers 24/7 connectivity via computer and personal digital assistant (PDA). Whether operating in borrowed or leased office space, a hotel room, or a pay telephone, with the properly equipped laptop and a fax/modem the mobile office–savvy public affairs practitioner can communicate efficiently and effectively virtually worldwide.

As an example of this concept, recently an organization was required to evacuate its headquarters facility for several days due to a fire in an adjacent structure. Because of extensive travel requirements, several senior executives were equipped with laptops, cellular telephones, and handheld organizers that allowed them to operate their mobile office while at remote sites. Immediately following the evacuation, these executives organized their staff in temporary quarters at five locations—which in three instances were in home offices or around dining room tables—and began the process of notifying stakeholders that they were conducting business as usual. Because their laptops and personal organizers used a "standard set" of software programs and could transfer information via infrared link, each team could establish a line-of-site wireless network that speeded the work process. In addition, using wireless communications capable PDAs, team members were able to maintain communications on the road.

The displaced crisis team first changed the switchboard voice mail message alerting callers to the emergency situation at their headquarters facility and a Web site that contained additional information prior to automatically forwarding the call to one of three sites. In addition, a special Web page advising stakeholders of the situation was developed, approved, and uploaded to the organization's Web server. Finally, an initial e-mail was drafted, edited, approved, and released to interested stakeholders and the media. All of these actions were "staffed to approval" via the telephone and e-mail. As the situation changed and more information was available, communication updates were made to the switchboard voice mail message, emergency Web page, and follow-up e-mails to stakeholders.

It is important to note that this contingency team had backed-up and carefully cataloged virtually all of its business information—customer data, graphics, accounting, Web sites, and other information—on Jaz disks. Following downloading onto a remote server, the team was able to proceed with business almost as usual. Without access to this critical data, the contingency team would have been unable to conduct business operations or communicate with their stakeholders.

As the situation dragged on, additional laptop computers, cellular telephones, and telephone lines were purchased to handle the volume of normal business. In addition to the extra telephone lines, conference calling and residential voice messaging services were purchased from the telephone company. After eight days, the organization was able to return to their headquarters facility and resume normal operations.

13.10   Contingency Public Affairs Office Equipment Checklist

The following is a comprehensive supply checklist required to equip a remote public affairs office. This checklist should be used as a *mix-and-match* to meet the nonprofit organization's contingency or remote requirements. Also, don't forget the option of using locally available vendors, public relations/advertising agencies, and other sources to provide some equipment and services required temporarily.

1. Public affairs equipment
   - Audiocassette tape recorder, handheld, with lectret condenser microphone
   - Videocassette recorder (¾-inch or ½-inch VHS)
   - Television receiver/monitor
   - Camera kit (35mm SLR), electronic flash unit, lenses (35mm/50mm/70–120mm zoom, or comparable), appropriate filters, tripod, case
   - Digital camera kit (35mm SLR), electronic flash unit, lenses (35mm/50mm/70–120mm zoom, or comparable), appropriate filters, tripod, case
   - Megaphone/hailer
   - Handheld communications system
   - Automatic broadcast feed unit
   - Cellular telephone
   - Portable lecterns (with built-in microphone/speakers/auxiliary inputs/outputs)
   - Media feed "multiboxes"
   - Portable mixers, extra microphones, power outlets, cables, and connectors
   - VHF/Bearcat frequency scanner
   - Radio, multiband, portable
   - Slide projector

- Overhead projector
- Screen
- Backdrop for briefings
- Chalkboard/bulletin board

2. Public affairs supplies
   - Audiocassette tapes (C-30 and C-60)
   - Videocassette tapes
   - Film, 35mm (Tri-X/Plus-X/color print/color slide)
   - Nicad batteries for camera and flash unit
   - Nicad batteries for tape recorders
   - Lettering/sign-making kit
   - Photo mailers
   - Cardboard photo protector
   - News release letterhead
   - Media center sign (with Velcro holder)
   - Nicad battery charger

3. Public affairs publications
   - Dictionary (English/Spanish/French/German)
   - Thesaurus (or comparable software program hard copy/floppy disk)
   - Public affairs staff directories
   - Ayers Dictionary of Publications
   - Regulations, instructions, directives (as appropriate)
   - Telephone directory
   - Maps/charts of area, including road map

4. Office furniture
   - Desks
   - Chairs
   - Computer desk/printer table
   - Filing cabinet, two-drawer
   - Light table

5. Office equipment
   - Laptop microcomputers with hard drive and fax modem
   - Backup system and application software
   - Backup files of all current work
   - Printers with cable connectors
   - Surge protector/fused electric cords
   - Facsimile/fax machine, portable
   - Typewriter, self-correcting electric, with various typewriter balls
   - Typewriter, manual
   - Telephone answering machine with audiocassette and audio patch cords
   - Xerographic copier, portable

6. Office supplies
    - Clipboards
    - Staplers
    - Staple remover
    - Scissors
    - Rulers (12- and 18-inch)
    - Pencil sharpener, electric
    - Pencil sharpener, manual
    - Hole punches (two- and three-hole)
    - File basket
    - Trash baskets
7. Office supplies (consumables)
    - Staples, rubber bands (various sizes), erasers, thumbtacks/push pins, pencils, ballpoint pens, felt tip pens (blue/black/red/green, etc.), waterproof felt tip markers (blue/black/red)
    - Masking tape (½-inch, 1-inch, 2-inch rolls)
    - Duct tape
    - Nylon filament tape
    - Cellophane tape (clear/transparent)
    - Clips, paper/binder
    - Bond paper (8 ½ × 11-inch)
    - Writing pads (legal pads, stenograph pads, carbon paper manifold sets, pocket pads, continuous form plain white computer paper, organization letterhead, labels)
    - Business envelopes, white manila (9 ½ × 12-inch, 6 × 9-inch)
    - Computer floppy diskettes (appropriate for type of laptop), hard/protected case labels
    - Telephone message pads
    - Address labels, gummed continuous form/fan-folded
    - 3 × 5-inch cards
    - Post-It™ notes
    - Name tags, individual, self-sticking, continuous-form
    - Telecopier paper
    - Fax paper
    - Index tabs
    - File folders
    - Accordion file folders
    - Glue sticks
    - Razor blades, single edge
    - Ribbons, typewriter and computer printer
    - Correction tape
    - Laser printer toner cartridges

8. Miscellaneous equipment
   - Heavy-duty worklight
   - Flashlights: three-cell, two-cell, penlight
   - Extension cords: 100-foot, 50-foot with multiple outlet strips
   - Coffee pot: 50-cup, including filters, coffee cups, sugar, cream substitute
   - Tool box with standard screwdrivers, Phillips screwdrivers, claw hammer, pliers, assorted
   - Nuts/bolts/nails/screws
9. Miscellaneous supplies
   - Nicad flashlight batteries ("D" and "C" sizes with recharger)
   - Insect repellent
   - Fly swatter
   - Broom
   - Cleaning supplies
10. Temporary shelter
    - Leased office space
    - Home office
    - Mobile home on site (office configuration)
    - Tent (large enough to accommodate 20 people plus equipment)

Note: Quantities of each item and actual items required will be determined by local requirements and expected duration.

Making Your Data Collection Meaningful (New)

Stephen Hobbs, EdD
WELLTH Learning Network

Dan R. Dyble, MSOD
WELLTH Learning Network

14A.13   Managing the Answers from the Questions

      Endnotes

14A.1   *Focus*

In writing this chapter, we are focusing on the management evaluation of data for volunteer resource managers (VRMs) involved in their volunteer resource management system (VRMS). The chapter provides an overview of the importance of *why* VRMs will need to collect data more than *how* to collect data. Also, the chapter prompts managers to think about what data they need to collect to comment on program success.

14A.2   *Overview*

Volunteer resource programs are being operated more and more with the techniques found in independent businesses. Within the nonprofit, voluntary sector, the shift to business acumen is referred to as social entrepreneurship. Using business tools and techniques, *social* entrepreneurs are innovating new solutions to community concerns.

     This transition is happening because of scarcity of resources and a desire to utilize available resources fully and effectively. As well, the managers of these programs are expected to make business-style presentations to those they seek resources from. This search for a more effective use of resources by VRMs within the community means effective program evaluation through data management is an indispensable component of a successful and sustainable program. It is the means by which VRMs can effectively communicate their program impacts and needs to those they approach for support both for funding and those being asked to volunteer their time and talents. Volunteer resource managers must select performance indicators that clearly demonstrate program quality and accountability to agency executives, external funders, volunteers, staff, and clients.

     The selected criteria are what those involved assess their program's success against. The criteria may be broken into key performance indicators (KPIs) that will represent the criteria in operational terms. Upon choosing the appropriate KPIs, VRMs must use these indicators to collect the data needed to communicate the value (worth, truth, and utility) of their programs. Prepared with their interpretation of data as information, VRMs are able to communicate effectively with all constituent groups. As if it was that easy.

     This chapter provides an overview of managing the evaluation of data; that is, the chapter outlines the importance of *why* VRMs will need to collect data and how to look at the role of data in their VRMS, more than *how* to collect data and design effective data collection tools. This chapter is concerned with data as a tool to manage, establish, and sustain a VRMS. Data is the input for creating information on which knowledge is generated. Without valid and reliable quantitative data and trustworthy and dependable qualitative data, the decisions that result may or may not do justice to what occurs.

     This chapter is not about the different types of tools and techniques used to collect data. Books and articles abound on the pros and cons surrounding each one and some in combination. Nor is the chapter outlining the merits of either qualitative or quantitative data. The only thing to say is both are necessary when collecting data.

14A.3   *Key Issues in Collecting Data*

Volunteer resource managers constantly search for data to create information and generate knowledge for proving something, improving something, and/or developing something of potential usefulness. They are in a constant search for program perspective that will lead them to both insight (within their program) and outsight (around their program).

The paramount demand VRMs make of the data they collect is whether it fits the purpose it needs to serve. Managers who reflect on the following concept stay ahead of the data-knowledge tension. "With the answers we are working with, are they to the questions we have asked?" Information derived from one situation may not be well suited to the next question asked. This data-knowledge tension is the gap between the data available and the knowledge desired. The gap is less as data creates information that generates knowledge.

The very act of collecting data, which is measuring/observing "something," alters the nature of that something being measured/observed. Whoever is collecting the data must be clearly and cleanly aware of what data is collected, pay attention to the people involved, and give intention to the choice of tool and techniques that arrives at the most appropriate response. Therefore, VRMs as practitioners involved in the data collecting must also be aware of the role they play in data collecting and the information and knowledge derived from the data collecting. Often, the act of asking a question can impact the awareness, focus, and action of those asked and those consuming the program offered.

The objective here is to undertake thematic, issue-based study using practitioner and practice-grounded inquiry.[1] From this study it is important for VRMs to develop a synergistic blend of qualitative and quantitative approaches, which are necessary for success in the short and long term.

Data collection must be understood clearly since accurate extrapolation is hazy at the best of times. Being clear about what you want to measure and possible biases that may arise as a result of your tools and techniques, and methodology and procedures, can make the difference between well-grounded, insightful data collection and a valiant effort with no substance.

(A)   FRAMING THE CHAPTER

With these key issues in the foreground, three essential questions frame this chapter:

1. What is data?
2. What is the management of data?
3. What is the evaluation of data?

To answer any one of these questions brings forth numerous perspectives. For the simple need to seek operational clarity, answers to these questions will provide VRMs with a reference point from which to determine both what information is required and who will use it. The focus of any data collection is to ensure the question being answered is the correct question being asked. Questions asked at different stages of a volunteer resource program can influence what data is possible to collect for creating information and where it can be used. A more established program may offer richer depth of data sources, while newer programs are often easier to incorporate data collection practices into.

14A.4   What Is Data?

Since the mid-1990s, when we asked VRMs the question "What is data?," there is sometimes an immediate and humorous reference to a human-like android character of Star Trek fame known as Data. He is an android struggling to understand humanity—what it is to be human. In keeping with this analogy, VRMs struggle with data to understand their programs' impact on humanity. Through data, VRMs inform themselves about what is happening on many levels.

Data is a collection of facts from which to draw conclusions—to create information as depicted in Exhibit 14A.1. The most common understanding of data is numeric. This is based on quantitative data. Often overlooked and undervalued is qualitative data—information conveying non-numeric, word/visual messages. These are considered more difficult to attain and summarize or understand.

Data collecting is essential for decision making and the actions that result from the decisions. As decisions are made, the VRMs are creating information that in turn becomes knowledge when acted on or potential knowledge when stored for later use. To make this connection between data-through-information-for-knowledge,

---

EXHIBIT 14A.1   **Placing Data in Context to Information and Knowledge**

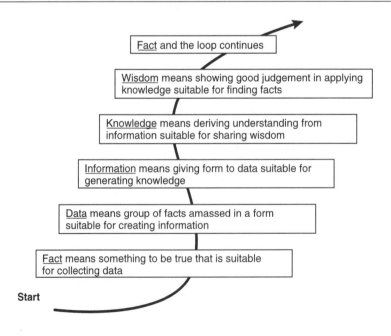

Fact and the loop continues

Wisdom means showing good judgement in applying knowledge suitable for finding facts

Knowledge means deriving understanding from information suitable for sharing wisdom

Information means giving form to data suitable for generating knowledge

Data means group of facts amassed in a form suitable for creating information

Fact means something to be true that is suitable for collecting data

Start

Hobbs[2] coined the term InformaCtion. While it is a visual play on words, significant meaning is derived from the use of the term.

In order to see ("*C*") the value of data (its worth, truth, and/or utility) as it translates into action and/or the potential for action requires the "creation of InformaCtion." That is, for VRMs who create information from collected data they can say "I *C* (I see), because I inform my aCtion." Also, the use of the word *creation* is purposeful in describing and explaining what occurs in collecting data for crafting information from and/or for a strategic perspective. Through the shift of the letter *c* in reaction to the front of the same word, you write the new word *creation*. Here, the meaning is "to see from different vantage points." When in the middle of program delivery, if a VRM chooses to collect data, it is most useful in the immediate and/or short term. Whereas if the VRM was to collect data for the purpose of creation, that is, to see what is needed in a strategic sense over the life of the program, then it is likely the data will have longer-term application.

Davis and Botkin[3] point out that between each of the words data, information, and knowledge (see Exhibit 14A.1) a "technology" exists. They found that between data collecting and information creating, technologies are clearly visible. They suggested that between information-creating and knowledge-generating, the technology is under investigation through the likes of information systems and knowledge management. We determine that between knowledge-generating and wisdom-sharing, an ever-present technology exists—that of "Conversation" with each other. Then it becomes critical to be mindful of what persons know as they share it with others. When VRMs are willing to share their learning-for-knowing in Conversation, they engage in dynamic dialogue with those involved in the VRMS. With wisdom-sharing to fact-finding, everyone involved must be observant that "when we speak, we educate; when we listen, we learn." One person's wisdom is another person's fact, and one VRM's wisdom is another VRM's fact.

(A) S-CURVE

Within Exhibit 14A.1 and in a simpler form in Exhibit 14A.2, the sigmoid or S-curve is used to indicate that the fact-to-wisdom path is a continuous loop. Handy[4] defines the sigmoid curve as "the S-shaped curve that has intrigued people since time

---

EXHIBIT 14A.2   Facts-to Wisdom Path

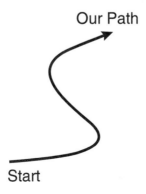

began. The sigmoid curve sums up the story of life itself. We start slowly, experimentally, and falteringly; we wax and then we wane."

Along its shape, product life cycles, innovation, and creativity have been explained and described over various time periods (e.g., computers over three years, social entrepreneurship over 10 or 20 years). One point, repeated in use of the S-curve, is to "start a new curve before the first one peters out."[5] Catching one's perspective on the topic of choice at the appropriate time along the curve, by starting another curve, offers one a path of least effort/more outcome in realizing and reframing that perspective. Within VRMS, programs and processes that are left without review will likely not operate as mapped. Programs that are reviewed internally based on what is happening externally (i.e., volunteers recruited versus clients to be served) can be adjusted to maximize delivery. The essential point here is to establish a new present-future (a forward looking perspective) to work through while always living in the past-present (having only the reality of the past and present to rely on for creating information). This situation describes and explains the *paradox of the present* given to everyone.

Mentioned already, the S-curve serves to display the direction, connection, and arrangement of facts, data, information, knowledge, and wisdom in ways that explain and describe the paradox of learning-for-knowing and the establishment of InformaCtion. These terms have great application in optimistically altering the VRMS. Facts about the VRMS are voiced and shown throughout the organization every day. When these facts are collected (data) and understood (information) in a way that allows the VRMS to shift the curve in the direction that will bring the most value to its stakeholders, then improvement is likely.

These facts abound in the everyday conversation of those involved in the VRMS. Each statement of opinion offered by a person is based on that person's perceived truth. While these statements, when taken one at a time, can inform a VRM's action, it is more prudent to collect many statements to ascertain what is happening/ what happened. This collective view offers the potential for an overall improvement in the VRMS organization and thus shifts the VRMS.

This shift in the VRMS is considered a transition. Hobbs & Karringten[6] refer to transition as "the gradual or sometimes sudden modification of your organizational (VRMS's) Current Reality into a noticeable and qualitatively different reality— your Vision." The challenge of transition is in how to bring it about or realize the VRMS's vision when all around the VRMS is change. Transition is achieved through a generative and iterative process appropriately described as *successive approximations.* These approximations are framed in three types of transition. They are called transaction, transformation, and transcendent transition.[7] Each is described as follows:

- *Transactional transition* is about doing the same thing better, where the main improvement is through administration and efficiency—doing things correctly.
- *Transformational transition* is about doing something else, where the main improvement is through management and effectiveness—doing correct things.
- *Transcendent transition* is about allowing for the unknown to happen, where the main improvement is through leadership and relevancy—doing things that matter.

The degree of shift is reflected in the data-to-knowledge tension.[8] Managing through a systems model to frame data collection facilitates evaluating the readiness of the VRMS for any given level of transition. Often it is possible to begin data collection before the VRMS is even begun or before a transition is made in how it is currently managed. Beginning data collection against appropriate criteria early on affords the VRMs the opportunity to look at longitudinal information or data that spans time and allow comparisons of snapshots of data at various stages of maturity of the program's life.

14A.5   What Is the Management of Data?

Management is about motivating and coordinating staff, volunteers, and clients toward the attainment of VRMS's goals and objectives. Planning is one example of many subtasks associated with management. Management ensures effectiveness in the VRMS by ensuring the correct things are done. Measurement of action is the data source from which management creates information for planning.

Below are working definitions of effectiveness that affect the VRMS. These are time related. Some are present each day, while others are extended over a year or more planning cycle.

In managing data there are two ways to work through the effectiveness diagram (see Exhibit 14A.3). Following the bold solid curve from bottom to top is the

---

EXHIBIT 14A.3   Levels of Effectiveness

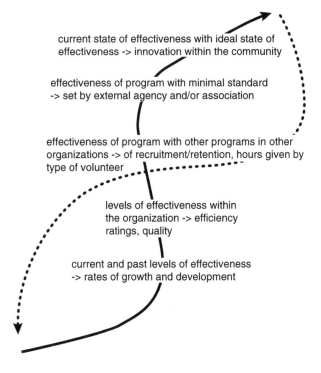

current state of effectiveness with ideal state of effectiveness -> innovation within the community

effectiveness of program with minimal standard -> set by external agency and/or association

effectiveness of program with other programs in other organizations -> of recruitment/retention, hours given by type of volunteer

levels of effectiveness within the organization -> efficiency ratings, quality

current and past levels of effectiveness -> rates of growth and development *briefing*—what will happen—format, while the dotted line coming down is the *debriefing*—what happened—with clarification of "so what" and "then what." Whichever starting point you choose, following the model will eventually lead you to follow the other half of the path. It is critical that both paths are completed in a continuous loop so as not to become stuck in the present. Volunteer resource managers need to consider the influence of past on present-to-future as they do future on present-from-past. This looping will lead the conversation with and about the VRMS through nonlinear and multidirectional paths where VRMs realize breakthroughs.

14A.6   Managing a Volunteer Resource Management System

Throughout this book and as supported by this chapter, a systems perspective or more important a systemic thinking approach is required to understand the VRMS. Systemic thinking[9] is about reflecting on thoughts and involvement with systems as a whole. That is, instead of thinking about who and what are involved as parts contributing to a whole (VRMS), each *who* and *what* are actually wholes contributing to a whole. A volunteer is a unique person who brings their experience to the VRMS. To treat these volunteers as the same lessens the potential for personal contribution and collective realization of the VRMS's vision. This revised thinking and involvement allows for understanding the wholes of the system that are cumulatively essential in the smooth implementation of the VRMS.

In Exhibit 14A.4, the system diagram is displayed in block style symbols. This portrayal affords a rigid picture of the VRMS. It is important to remember that no system that has human interactions involved is static. Volunteer resource managers must recognize the dynamic nature of their VRMS so they acknowledge that the *post* of one moment (output) is the *pre* of the next (input). What a volunteer has to say during an exit interview is useful data to inform the VRM on how to improve the VRMS.

EXHIBIT 14A.4   System Model with Time Orientation

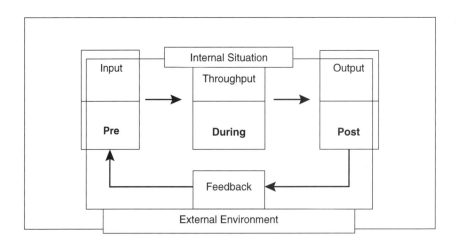

The pre, during, and post time designations in Exhibit 14A.4 were used by Hobbs[10] in listing the components of a VRMS. By components we mean recruitment, orientation, training, exit interviews, and the like where the recruitment component is listed under the *pre* designation while exit interviews are listed under the *post* designation. These three time designations and the accompanying statements that follow provide reference points from which to manage the collection of data. These statements are like the subject matter captured in photography. Similar to a photograph, whose subject is appreciate through review, the collected data are snapshots of the VRMS that can be analyzed and synthesized to provide insight and/or outsight. This review contributes to understanding the volunteer resources program that, in turn, allows for smooth(er) operation of the VRMS.

Pre

- Manage volunteers—obtain as contributors to programs with staff
- Manage staff—for support of volunteers in programs
- Manage internal situation—availability of resources and technology
- Manage identification of program strategic, structural, and relational issues
- Manage external environment—matching organizational mission (program—product, service, and experience delivery) with community needs
- Manage management practices (with volunteers and staff) and program principles (with clients and other organizational staff)

During

- Manage volunteers—as they contribute to programs with staff
- Manage staff—as they support volunteers in programs
- Manage internal situation—use of resources including technology
- Manage initiatives for resolving program strategic, structural, and relational issues
- Manage formative evaluation of programs—internal situation assessment
- Manage formative evaluation of program outcomes—external environment appraisal
- Manage formative evaluation of management practices and program principles

Post

- Manage volunteers as they continue or leave programs
- Manage staff as they continue or leave programs
- Manage internal use of resources in continuation and/or termination of programs
- Manage review of resolution of strategic, structural, and relational issues
- Manage summative evaluation of internal situation view of program products, services, and experience

- Manage summative evaluation of external environment view of program outcomes
- Manage summative evaluation of management practices and program principles

From this list, whether the data is collected from those inside the program (volunteers, workers, and clients) or from those outside the program (sponsors, related programs, and the general public) it provides both inside-out and outside-in perspectives. These perspectives allow a glimpse of how the program works as seen by both insiders and outsiders. Even being aware of the difference in evaluation from inside and outside sources can give valuable clues as to the successful coordination and general/specific trends which may help predict needed transition in program direction and commitment.

The boundary line of any VRMS as suggested by inside–outside delineation is used to distinguish the internal situation and external environment of the system. The internal situation of the VRMS is defined by the demarcation placed on the VRMS as a department of the organization and/or as a support function to the program services offered by the organization. Whatever the distinction, what lies outside the boundary is the external environment. In large hospitals, for example, the boundary delineation of a VRMS may include departments and possibly the community as a whole. With smaller organizations, the entire organization can be viewed as the internal situation of the VRMS because the small staff all manage the volunteer management system.

With the internal situation, it is important for those involved to understand what management practices are in use. In other words, how will the system be managed? Also, it is important to understand what program principles are to be used with clients or other organizations. In dealing with clients, one organization will ask clients to come to them whereas in another organization the volunteers go to the clients. Either arrangement with clients has impact on volunteer involvement, the management system that supports them, and the data to be collected.

Within the internal situation, there are ongoing strategic, structural, and relational issues that need to be identified, and initiatives taken to resolve these issues. The various chapters in this book highlight different ways to deal with these three issues and their combinations. Also, the search for appropriate physical resources including technology is a challenge every day. Add to this challenge a search for the volunteers and staff that complement organizational programs, then the VRMS is dynamic indeed.

14A.7   When Managing the Systems Approach

When managing the systems approach, the following characteristics are ever present to the VRM. Understanding them provides a step up in managing the VRMS. Some characteristics are evident immediately, while others take time to realize:

- *What* happens externally influences internal operations more than *What* happens internally influences the external environment.
- Many program outputs are used as inputs.
- Everything is interrelated.

- Programs are constantly transitioning.
- The culture of the program is important.
- The culture of the organization is important.
- Any level within a program can be viewed as a system.
- A system ensures data.

Data collection is not a random management act. It must be thought through and coordinated. Therefore, it is important to be clear in the direction of data collection and the tools best suited. Below are data characteristics we have found important for VRMs to consider in order to develop a credible data foundation from which to create information.

14A.8   Data Considerations

Knowing the VRMS ensures access to a constant stream of facts, it is important to know the following about managing for and from data. This section was adapted from Hauser and Katz's[11] work on metrics:

- *Collect data that can be understood today and that impacts future results.* Collect present data for future decisions because past archival data offers a past perspective like recruitment/retention ratio by month.
- *Ensure that the collection of data is in the control of those who collect the data.* Where there is risk involved in data collection, those involved in collecting may or may not do it as desired depending on how they personally view risk.
- *Exploit all ideas around the interpretation of data while balancing the influence of quantitative and qualitative data.* The story is told in a variety of ways like numbers, words, drawings, and the like.
- *Ensure that decisions made to use data are the same decisions used to move VRMS in the same direction.* Using data about growth when you are attempting to downsize a volunteer program is counterproductive.
- *Choose data that are accurate, sometimes at the expense of preciseness—collect what is important.* Sometimes subjective interpretation of data is important especially in recruiting volunteers—the manager seeing the shyness of a volunteer who may have been rejected yet could turn out to be a wonderful library volunteer who over time can blossom into a wonderful support services volunteer.
- *Identify data that allow everyone to work smarter not harder.* If collecting the data means extra work, then it may not get done properly. Be clear what value the people who are collecting the data place on the data. Volunteer resource managers must understand the jobs through which data are collected. When the effort put into collecting data is part of the workers' perspective of their time and effort associated with the job, then in the short term they will complete all tasks. However, eventually something has to give or go. When data are perceived as too much work, then they go. Remember, collecting data does not come free.

- *Include data collection into your VRMS business principles and management practices on a daily basis.* By including it, you will engender the terms and thought processes into your conversation about your VRMS.
- *Fold your arms the other way when considering data of choice.* Too often data are chosen in too narrow a view because the VRM may be focused on measuring volunteer involvement in a program—What are volunteers doing?—when the more important question may well be—Do we need volunteers in the program?
- *Determine who the data belong to.* Are they for the volunteer resources program, the staff, the organization, the volunteers, or the clients served by the volunteers? Develop data around the needs of the users of the data—for volunteers the data may be "Is it easy to get involved?"; for the staff, "Are there qualified volunteers available?"; for clients, "Can the volunteer I speak with be qualified to handle my question?" In other words, involve those involved in using the data in the data collection.
- *Ask those involved to test the data before assigning the data collection in full.* Ask those involved to provide feedback on the applicability of the data and its influence on the work of the person. Those involved are practitioners most closely aligned with collecting the data and can offer thoughts on what works and what does not. Their involvement in a test case can speak volumes to an overall application.

However, it is important to recognize that the potential for conflict exists when managing data collection because:

- Data that shows growth can lead to less decision making, reduced efficiency, and less ability to adjust to environmental changes.
- People can live (work) with conflicting priorities surrounding data collection because they do not bring priorities and data together.
- Collected data does not meet the needs of everyone.
- Debates occur when collecting qualitative and/or quantitative data. Therefore, deciding the rigor of data collection necessary is important before collecting the data. It is imperative this decision is made beforehand and not while collecting the data and certainly not after collecting the data. If rigor is high, employ the appropriate data collection by appropriate criteria. If rigor is less, make a judgement and make sure to declare your position.

Much of the conflict can be managed by being mindful of the conversation (the questions asked) about data collection. Clarity of personal and VRMS's goals and objectives help VRMs recognize their biases that affect their listening for learning. In asking questions, VRMs will discover VRMS issues in a nonconfrontational and embracing way. This question approach allows VRMs and their team to hear the potential solutions framed as answers. Allowing the question to confront the respondents rather than people confronting each other redirects the emotional charge from a negative interpersonal debate to a positive solutions required dialogue.

14A.9　*Typical Questions to Ask When Managing Data Collection*

The following list is a composite of important questions to ask when managing data collection.

(A) DATA VALUE

- Why is the data being collected?
- What is the fit of data collection in your VRMS?

Potential Responses:

- Deal with operation issues, funder requirements, and so on.

> To start: Create your key performance indicators that are *Specific, Measurable, Attainable, Realistic,* and *Time* defined to ensure *Effectiveness* and *Relevance* (S.M.A.R.T.E.R.)

(B) DATA LEVEL

- What level is the data to be collected?

Potential Responses:

- Mega, macro, micro

> To start: Define the boundary of your VRMS (whole organization, department in the organization, etc.), then determine the depth of competence for data collection within and around the bounded area. This level of competence will determine the preparedness for collecting data at a given depth.

(C) DATA DIRECTION

- In what direction is the data to be collected?

Potential Responses:

- In → out, out → in

> To start: After defining your boundary, consider the strengths of collecting data from the outside in or inside out. Often, the perspectives of those within and outside the boundary differ and when seen together tell a more complete story.

(D) DATA COLLECTION APPROACH

- How will the data be collected?

Potential Responses:

- Research different approaches like action research to questionnaires to interviews to observation studies to practitioner reflection.

> To start: The nature of the data being collected determines the approach that is most appropriate. A questionnaire for exit interviews versus a one-on-one conversation interview results in creating different information. The approach influences people's willingness to participate and supply data.

(E) DATA REVIEW

- Is the data primary or secondary to your work?

Potential Responses:

- Primary
- Secondary
- Combination

> To start: As you go about your work, determine whether the data you collect is primary (i.e., it influences you in the moment) or secondary (i.e., you analyze it later) or you may do a combination of both. Frequently, what is primary in one situation is secondary for another, and vice versa.

(F) DATA ANALYSIS

- Is the data appropriate to the situation?
- Who will review the data?
- Who is affected by the data?

Potential Responses:

- Look within the VRMS for staff and volunteers as well as funders and clients, and other programs, their staff, and volunteers.

> To start: As you consider the data collected, does it answer the question being asked? Often, we use answers to different questions that lead us on serendipitous trips. Then, are those reviewing the data bringing a fresh perspective for creating information? Again, of those reviewing the data are they highlighting the opportunities or the limitations inherent in the data.

(G) DATA INTEGRITY

- Is the data recoverable?
- Is the data trustworthy?

Potential Responses:

- Recoverable
- Trustworthy

> To start: Having collected the data, can you replicate it again should it be destroyed or compromised? Also, are those collecting data capable of collecting data at the specified competency levels?

(H) DATA REPORTING

- What format will be used to report the data?

Potential Responses:

- The format influences the message (e.g., briefing paper, handout, formal report, software reports). Often this cannot be decided until the story of data collection is complete.

> To start: Consider the way the data will be portrayed for ease of creating information.

(I) DATA CLEANUP

- What approach will be used to clean up the data?
- What approach is available to avoid data pollution?

Potential Responses:

- Consider hand developed versus computer assisted; consider how many people can influence data collection and the impacts this may have.

> To start: Be mindful of collection, analysis, and reporting biases of those involved—yourself and your supervisor included.

(J) DATA TO INFORMATION

- What decision making surrounds data for the purpose of creating information upon which action will be taken?

Potential Responses:

- Given the answers to the question asked, what action are we prepared to take to realize the VRMS vision?

To start: With the vision in mind, take the data that frames information and decide your VRMS strategic direction, relational connections, and structural arrangement in which key issues are identified and priority initiatives are implemented.

14A.10   What Is the Evaluation of Data?

Evaluation is about continuously improving the operations of the VRMS. Evaluation aims to ensure reasonableness (fair, not extreme) by ensuring that the correct things are and were improved. For the VRMs it becomes a question of determining worth of their VRMSs. That is, when VRMs evaluate, they determine the worth of the program to those involved.

From understanding this worth of existing programs (to improve the programs), it is possible to understand the truth (to prove the usefulness) and the utility (the potential that can develop from the program). From understanding the worth, truth, and utility of existing programs, there is the potential to create new programs and breathe new life into existing ones.

14A.11   Four Levels of Data Evaluation

Many writers have written about evaluation of programs. Each has its merits. However, we return to Kirkpatrick's[12] four distinct levels of evaluation. His deceptively simple method of evaluating training has been adapted in this chapter as it relates to the evaluation of VRMS data. See Exhibit 14A.5.

Kirkpatrick maintains that different methods of gathering data are used at each level. He suggests that data gathered at one level tells little or nothing about success at another level. For example, volunteers at level 1 might tell their VRM they loved the trainer, had a good time, and found the session interesting. This data tells the VRM little or nothing about level 3. Volunteer resource managers must find a means to assess volunteers' behavior to determine if the training is effective.

Typically, the data garnered at level 1 is easier to collect and harder to quantify. For example, four out of five volunteers may have reported finding their training as interesting and valuable, but since a VRM does not know what the volunteers might be using as criteria for valuable, the results are very subjective (personal opinion). By the time VRMs are evaluating at level 4, they will know if volunteers found the training valuable through the observable behaviors—if they are doing what was taught, then training was valuable; if they are not, then something has not been completed. Either the training was not on target, the volunteers did not find it practical when they got to apply it (often this is due to something else in the system making the training less than easy to apply), or the culture of the organization does not encourage integration of new practices. There are many possible ex-

EXHIBIT 14A.5   Levels of Data Collection

Level 1	Reaction Data	Data collected that asks for an immediate response from stakeholders. This is data collected during the exit interview, at the end of programs, solicited responses to budget presentations at board meetings where those involved provide a response according to a rating scale, a thumbs up, thumbs down, and/or voicing their level of satisfaction by nodding yes or no.
Level 2	Learning Data	With this level you need to determine if those involved actually learned about what they participated in while listening, actively doing, etc. In other words, can they educate others about what they learned, that is, can the data they collected be turned into information for them?
Level 3	Behavior Data	Those involved in data collection go about their work because they are informed because of the data they collect. This is where those involved actually use the data to the benefit of themselves and those they interact with on a personal level.
Level 4	Results Data	At this level, the data collected assesses the benefits to the organization as a collective. Those involved are performing their tasks with improvement because of the data they are collecting. Here, data collected from other parts of the organization can be shared to determine improvement in delivery and increase in value of the VRMS. Also, there is great tangibility of the data—reliability and validity for quantitative data and trustworthiness and dependability for qualitative data.

planations as to why the results fall where they do. Selecting the appropriate data level for inquiry helps to establish the level of information the VRM can draw from the data.

14A.12   Selection of Questions for Which Data Can Be Collected

The type of data to be collected is listed below. By no means is this list exhaustive. It is merely illustrative and a beginning for VRMs' development of a "data-to-be-collected-list." The list is also framed as questions for reasons explained above. A question requires an answer whereas a data criteria statement seems unfinished; that is, it is unclear what is to be done with the criteria. Most questions can be asked at any of the four evaluation levels. Often, what determines the level is the type of data requested. If a behavioral level answer is requested, or when in the program the data is collected and from whom it is gathered affects your choice of question by evaluation level, ask a level 3 or 4 question. A new volunteer at the beginning of a program has a different perspective/ability from the 20-year volunteer in a long-standing program.

(A) RESOURCES

- What types of revenues support the VRMS?
- What level of allocation is made to the VRMS from the revenues?
- How many volunteers are involved by job category?
- How many volunteers are considered full time? Part time?
- What is the social background of volunteers?
- What is the social background of staff?
- What level of training and education do existing volunteers and staff have?
- What is the reputation of volunteers and staff involved in the VRMS?
- What measure of innovation is applied to VRMS volunteers and staff?
- How useful is the database?
- Does the database support effective management of volunteers?

(B) RELATIONSHIPS

- What pattern of decision making is evident among the volunteers, between staff and volunteers, and among staff?
- Who is involved in strategy formulation for the VRMS?
- What types of conflicts exist in the VRMS? How are these conflicts managed?
- Are staff and volunteers involved in issue identification and initiative resolution?
- What are the preferred communication styles among those involved (oral, written, meetings, etc.)
- What volunteer resource procedures exist to complement the corresponding policies?

(C) RESULTS

- What is the mix of services/products provided through the VRMS?
- What is the quantitative measure of service/products?
- What are the results of the quality indicators—reputation, ratings, complaints?
- What are the results of the human involvement indicators—absenteeism, turnover?
- What type of volunteer involvement (long, short, episodic) occurs?

(D) STRUCTURE

- In what areas of the organization is the VRMS active?
- How many levels of hierarchy are involved in VRMS?
- What is the basis for groupings of those involved in and through VRMS? Are the governance volunteers supported by the VRMS?

- What is the span of control of the VRMS staff and volunteers?
- What are the formal obligations affecting the VRMS?
- Where are the VRMS offices placed within the organization?

(E) TECHNOLOGY

- What is the level of VRMS automation?
- Is the data management (information) system working to the benefit of those involved?
- Is form control technologically reviewed and updated?

(F) INTERNAL SITUATION

- What priority is given to the VRMS and its program in relation to other programs in the organization?
- What level of autonomy is given to volunteers and staff as they complete their job tasks?
- What level of linkage exists between VRMS and other departments/programs?
- What level of well-living workplace have we achieved for our volunteers? Our staff? Our customers interacting with our staff and volunteers?
- What types of decor, symbols, and the like describe and explain our VRMS programs?
- What myths, rituals, dominant styles of dress display our commitment to action?
- What type of work style is expected in the VRMS (i.e., overtime, taking work home)?
- What is the perception of legitimacy for the VRMS to exist within the organization?
- What is the level of achievement for stated objectives?
- Have we initiated any breakthorough programming? What was the level of reception?
- How have we improved the program?
- Are the volunteers achieving their personal objectives?
- Is more training needed?
- Is there adequate trained staff?
- Does our training work?
- Are there adequate physical and financial resources?
- What draws volunteers to our organization?
- Are we serving the desired/expected number of clients?
- Do the clients we attract fit the profile we had expected?
- Are the client's needs from the program changing?

(G) EXTERNAL ENVIRONMENT

- What are the funding sources for VRMS?
- What is our description of social surroundings affecting us?
- What type of relationship do we foster with associations like our local chapter of volunteer managers and national organizations like Association for Volunteer Administration?
- What level of interaction do we have with other VRMS in other organizations?
- What is our articulated social responsibility for our program? Our organization?
- What is our impact on nature?
- Is the program seen as meeting a need in the community?
- Are those who sponsor it satisfied their resources are being applied appropriately?
- What is keeping resources from us, that is, why do some people not volunteer, donate, and the like?
- Where can this program have the greatest impact?

(H) PROGRAM DYNAMICS

- What is our program life cycle?
- Do we operate through an intrapreneurial and/or entrepreneurial format?
- What level of formalization surrounds our work?
- Do we encourage person in collective?
- Do we decide through a values-based approach where we are clear about our expressed ethics?
- Have we articulated and lived our management practices?
- Have we articulated and shared our business principles?

(I) STRATEGY

- What is our mission and vision for VRMS?
- What is the level of realization of VRMS's mission and vision?
- How do the VRMS mission and vision contribute to our organization's mission and vision?
- What is the level of realization of our program goals and objectives?

14A.13   *Managing the Answers from the Questions*

The answers to selected questions provide the VRM with data outlined at one or more of the four levels. The task at hand is to manage the VRMS from these answers to ensure that those involved clearly understand the worth, truth, and utility surrounding the VRMS. Often, persons act on answers to questions not asked.

This confusion is like taking serendipitous trips. While fun, they may not get you where you desire.

The key management practice for every VRM is to ask the appropriate questions to obtain answers from those involved. Working from the answers to the selected questions contributes to comprehending the direction, arrangement, and connection for those involved. From this comprehension, those involved in the VRMS are better able to manage program strategies, structures, and relationships. All of this work fosters the vision of the VRMS. In this way, the VRMS is seen to improve the value of the organization through improvement in the delivery of its programs.

No VRMS exists in a static environment. From a systems perspective the VRMS is open, alive, and evolving. Therefore, even though VRMs can make data collection an iterative part of the VRMS, it is important to match how to collect data within the shifting culture of the VRMS and the organization as a whole.

Endnotes

1. Wood, M. M. (1993). "Using Practitioners' Theories to Document Program Results," *Nonprofit Management and Leadership* 4(1): 85–106.
2. Hobbs, S., and G. Grant. (1998). "The S-Curve Relevance to Collective Learning for Knowing Using TRACE Participatory Action Research." In *Proceedings of the 17th Annual Conference of Canadian Association for the Study of Adult Education.* Ottawa: Canadian Association for the Study of Adult Education, pp. 134–38.
3. Davis, S., and J. Botkin. (1994). *The Monster Under the Bed: How Business is Mastering the Opportunity of Knowledge for Profit.* New York: Simon & Schuster.
4. Handy, C. (1994). *The Age of Paradox.* Boston, MA: Harvard Business School Press, p. 50.
5. Id., p. 51.
6. Hobbs, S., and D. Karringten. (2001). *Cultural Transition: Exploring Transition-based Organization through TRASE©.* Calgary, AB: The International Institute for Cultural Transition, p. 38.
7. Id., p. 38.
8. Id., p. 74.
9. Flood, R. L. (1999). *Rethinking the Fifth Discipline: Learning Within the Unknowable:* London: Routledge.
10. Hobbs, S. (1999). "Training, Education and Development Management Map (TEDMM): Identifying Learning Needs of Volunteers." In T. D. Connors (ed.), *The Nonprofit Handbook* (2nd ed., supplemental). New York: John Wiley & Sons, pp. 73–91.
11. Hauser, J. R., and G. M. Katz. (1998). "Metrics: You Are What You Measure!" *European Management Journal,* 16(5): 516–28.
12. Kirkpatrick, D. L. (1998). *Evaluating Training Programs: The Four Levels.* San Francisco: Berrett-Koehler.

PART II

Efficiency

REVENUE GENERATION

SYLVIA ALLEN, President, Allen Consulting

19A.1 Introduction: How to Get Started

As managers, leaders, and fund raisers in the nonprofit field, you are accustomed to asking for money. You produce events for fund raisers, you send out direct-mail solicitations, you apply for grants, and you court and nurture your major donors. You have been successful using traditional fund-raising strategies and tactics.

However, you could be more successful if you step into the for-profit world and understand how to sell.

First, *sales* is not a dirty word. Most people, when hearing the word *salesman,* cringe and conjure up an image of a sleazy used-car salesman in a pinstriped suit, with a smarmy smile and an overly zealous handshake. You may envision him as clever, cunning, a liar, a cheat, someone who will do anything to make the sale. That is *not* a salesperson, that's just a sleazy operator! A *good* salesperson is a consultant—someone who is concerned about the customers' wants and needs and makes every effort to satisfy those needs. The good salespeople are investigative and obliging and sublimate their own needs and desires for those of their customer.

Why do you need to know this information? As you are well aware, it is getting increasingly difficult to raise money because there is more competition for the same dollars, our economy is impacting people's abilities to give, and the traditional avenues—foundation grants and government and local funding—are not generating the same dollars as in the past. Understanding effective sales techniques, plus knowing how and when to approach individuals and organizations, will give you an "edge" over others who continue to follow the traditional paths.

In this section we will discuss the various qualities of good salespeople, different selling techniques, and how to apply it to revenue generation. After reading this section, you should be able to apply professional selling techniques to your fund-raising efforts and increase your effectiveness (through increased revenue) at generating money for your nonprofit organization.

However, before you start selling you should understand the sales process. It requires sensitivity to the needs of your donors as well as a complete understanding of the benefits you offer through your organization. These benefits, which you have previously considered to be primarily the value of a charitable contribution, go beyond that for today's donors. There are emotional benefits to helping others less fortunate than yourself, there are corporate benefits associated with cause-related marketing, and there are marketing benefits that accrue to an organization as a result of making contributions to nonprofit organizations. Your sales skills are important, whether you are doing basic fund raising or sponsorship.

19A.2   What's the Difference between Sponsorship and Fund Raising?

As more and more nonprofits discover that fund raising is not giving them a sufficient return on their invested efforts, they are considering alternative ways of generating revenue for their particular cause. One of the ways available to them is sponsorship, but what is sponsorship and how does it differ from fund raising?

First, the term *fund raiser* is primarily used by nonprofit organizations and, more specifically, those designated as 501(c)(3) by the Internal Revenue Service. Seldom will you find a fund raiser in a for-profit organization. This term is used when a donation is made and there is no marketing value as a result of the donation.

Second, sponsorship is used primarily when discussing money invested in an event, an activity, or an organization that has some form of payback whether it be improved media relations, enhanced sales, increased product visibility, or any of a number of marketing components that enhance the sponsoring organization's marketing efforts.

Third and last, the goals are the same—to raise money. The target companies are the same; the contact people in those companies are totally different. The approach, strategies, and tactics are totally different. The following is a brief look at each and a summary of the respective approaches.

(A) FUND RAISING

Both the mindset and process contrast sharply with the sponsorship approach. For fund raising, using the medium of direct marketing (either direct mail or telemarketing), the fund raiser puts together an "appeal"—asking for money—and then sends it out to a target audience. There is no direct one-on-one selling and the fund raiser is apologetic for his or her approach. The primary benefit to a company giving a donation to a fund raiser, besides helping a worthy cause, is the tax deductibility of the contribution.

(B) SPONSORSHIP

Conversely, for sponsorship the approach is highly targeted where sponsor wants and needs are matched carefully to event/organization opportunities so both sides benefit. The sponsorship salesperson meets with the sponsor and discusses the benefits to be realized from sponsorship and works with that sponsor on cross-promotions, exposure, and measurement criteria. The benefit to the company investing in a sponsorship is mutually decided between the sponsorship company and sponsored organization. This could include increased sales, enhanced product exposure, or improved employee relations.

(C) SUMMARY

Which one offers more? They both have value and, if combined, offer a sponsor the synergy of being associated with a worthwhile cause (cause-related marketing [CRM]) and a marketing investment that provides a measurable return. The convergence of fund raising and sponsorship is win–win for *all* parties involved.

(D) RELATED THINKING

Sponsorship? Charitable contribution? Corporate philanthropy? Does it matter what we call it? Of course it does—enormously. All those who seek funding had best know which corporate pocket they are targeting. The request for a donation is vastly different from the proposal for a sponsorship relationship. The contact point is different; the goals are different; the language is different.

It matters, too, on the corporate side because of the widely differing goals of the donations committee, for example, and the brand management team. The opportunity for leverage is the single largest loss that comes from corporate confusion about the differences between sponsorship and charity.

Are there hybrids? Of course there are. Especially where large sums or complex funding requirements are involved, or where a corporation continues under the leadership of a founding entrepreneur who is likely to make personal decisions on both sponsorships and charitable contributions.

Exhibit 19A.1 provides a quick overview of the differences between sponsorship and charitable contributions.

EXHIBIT 19A.1   Sponsorship versus Charitable Contributions

	Sponsorship	Charitable Contribution
Publicity	Highly public	Usually little widespread fanfare
Source	Typically from marketing, advertising, or communications budgets	From charitable donations or philanthropy budgets
Accounting	Written off as a full business expense, like promotional printing expenses or media from placement expenses	Write-off is limited to 75% of net income. This limit was increased 20% earlier this year. As a result, accounting/tax considerations are less likely to influence the way a corporation designates funding of a nonprofit organization
Objectives	To sell more products/services; to increase positive awareness in markets and amongst distant stakeholders (customers, potential customers, geographic community)	To be a good corporate citizen; to enhance the corporate image with closest stakeholders (employees, shareholders, suppliers)
Partner/recipient	Events; teams, arts, or cultural organizations; projects; programs. A cause is sometimes associated with the undertaking	Larger donations are typically cause-related (education, health, diseases, disasters, environmental), but can also be cultural, artistic, or sports related. At times, funding is specifically designated for a project or programs; at times, it is provided for operating budgets
Where most funding goes	Sports gets the lion's share of sponsorship dollars— around 65%	Education, social services, and the health sector get 75% of charitable donations

19A.3   Getting Started

The selling process consists of a number of steps, many of which you should already be doing to ensure that your fund-raising efforts are successful. The selling process consists of the following nine steps:

1. Networking
2. Researching
3. Cold calling
4. Appointment setting
5. Interview process
6. Closing
7. Contracts, letters of agreement, commitments, payment plans, and the like
8. Servicing/Record keeping
9. Repeat business

(A) NETWORKING

Where do you find your leads for potential donors? Most of you rely on referrals from your board of directors, other donors, or friends. However, you could expand your donor base by getting out to organizational meetings, other events similar to yours, or cross-marketing with other organizations similar to yours. Remember to always introduce yourself; never do a sales pitch in the social setting and just get a business card or contact name/number. You can follow up later. Your whole goal in the networking process is just to get leads that can be followed up later.

(B) RESEARCHING

Know who your prospects are before you make any telephone calls. (See Section 19A.4 for one source of information—Annual Reports.) In addition to corporate information that is available through annual reports and on the Internet, you can get additional personal information just by asking people. Ask the people who referred this door to you for a profile on the person. For example, what is their giving pattern, what do they support (or what does their company support), and so on. The more knowledge you have, the better prepared you are to discuss the value of their participation in your nonprofit.

(C) COLD CALLING

When making telephone calls, be prepared to run into problems. You could end up with a very powerful gatekeeper who won't put you through; you could encounter voice mail that blocks your call. Some tips for reaching your prospect: If calling at work, call before 8 AM or after 5 PM even on Saturday morning. These are less hectic times of the day and your prospective donor is likely to be more responsive to your telephone call.

Once you have identified yourself, don't launch into a long "commercial" for your nonprofit organization. Rather, lead with several questions that will invoke "yes" responses. If this is a personal referral, "Do you know _____?" In other words, establish rapport and get them to "yes." After a couple of those types of questions, tell them you would like to have just a few moments of their time to demonstrate how their participation in your nonprofit can benefit them/their company. If they ask you to send something, agree to send just a one-page fact sheet (Would they like to receive it by fax or e-mail?) and tell them that you will provide them with more extensive information when you meet. Try to set the appointment then. If that doesn't work, send the information via fax or e-mail.

(D) APPOINTMENT SETTING

Immediately after faxing or e-mailing the information, contact the prospect for an appointment. Ask them if they would like to meet on Monday or Friday (Which is better for you, morning or afternoon?) Always give choices; don't say, "Would you like to meet?" because the answer is automatically "no." If you give choices it becomes very difficult for them to refuse to meet with you. Keep in mind that these are busy people. Offer to meet them for breakfast, after work, or on Saturday. Meet with them at *their* convenience, not yours.

(E) INTERVIEW PROCESS

This is where your research pays off. You can have a discussion with your prospects about their businesses, their involvement with various nonprofit organizations, and how their affiliation with you is important. This is when you can detail what your organization does and how it impacts society. Again, tie it to the needs, goals, and objectives of your prospect so that the affiliation is logical. If you have done your research, this is a logical and simple process.

(F) CLOSING

No matter how charming you are and how wonderful the meeting, you do come to the moment when you have to ask for money. Don't just thank them for their time, leave material for them to read, and then walk away praying that they will offer something. You have to ask, "What level of contribution had you planned?" In fact, it is not out of line to suggest a specific dollar amount ("May I assume, Mr. Jones, that your contribution will be in the $10,000 range?"), and ask them how they want to pay it. Would they like to give you a check, put it on a credit card, or be invoiced? You have to ask and, of course, that is the most difficult part of the process, because the person could say "no." However, as a salesperson, that is the gamble. If you have done a good job of explaining value and benefits, have understood your potential donor, and have spoken to him or her in his or her language, the odds are very good that you will be successful in your efforts. Understand that there are several rules of selling. One is you have to get to five "nos" before you get to yes, and you have to make 100 calls to get 10 appointments to get one sale. So don't give up after the first no and don't give up after 89 bad calls! (As you get better at selling, your odds will improve.)

(G) CONTRACTS, LETTERS OF AGREEMENT, COMMITMENTS, PAYMENT PLANS, AND THE LIKE

Once you have the commitment, follow through on your end. Send the commitment letter, send the invoice, send the contract—whatever they requested—in a timely fashion. Be prompt in your response.

(H) SERVICING/RECORD KEEPING

Now, after getting the money don't ignore your donors. Put them on your newsletter mailing list, call them quarterly to tell them what's happening, and invite them to a function where they can meet other donors. In other words, consider this function customer service. Don't think that a once a year contact will be your most productive. The more you communicate with the donors, the more likely you are to continue getting donations as well as getting an increase. Good salespeople service their clients and continue to get additional money from them if they are doing so properly.

(I) REPEAT BUSINESS

If you service the donors, provide them with ongoing communications, and nurture the relationship, you can be fairly certain that they will continue giving and often will increase their giving because you have demonstrated that you care about them.

Follow these basic steps and you will be a successful fund raiser because you will have followed the fundamental rules of good selling.

The following sections provide you with specific information as they relate to various steps in the sales process as just listed, as well as good advice on how to be an effective salesperson.

19A.4 Why Use Annual Reports?

This relates to Step 2 in the sales process—researching. Good salespeople do their homework before calling on a donor or a company. One of the easiest ways to get information is to read the annual report to get a sense of what the company is doing.

Annual reports showcase a company to its customers and stockholders. The introduction sets up the rest of the report by making a good first impression. It often features a letter from the chairman to the stockholders describing the previous year and plans for the future. By reading this section closely, you can generally figure out what the company considers important, what is happening that's exciting, and what problems the company expects to face. Look for the company overview as well as important information about the company's structure, markets, products, and customers.

Finally, just before the financial information you will find a more objective explanation of operating results. A word of caution: Companies want to use the introduction to paint as flattering a picture of the company as possible. As you read, look for the following information:

- *Vision or mission statement.* Mission statements can help galvanize and unify employees for a common goal. Also, if the company makes purchasing decisions with its mission in mind, you need to know what that mission is.

- *Strategies for achieving the mission.* These plans should tell you a little about the economic constraints of the business environment and describe how the company will use its resources to gain a competitive edge and reach its goals. Most companies list between three and five specific business strategies. Analyze them carefully and decide how your nonprofit organization helps the company with their business strategies.

- *Principal lines of business.* Many large companies actually comprise several businesses rolled into one. The more you know about the different businesses they are in, the more selling opportunities you may find. Pay close attention to recent acquisitions to find out where the company is headed and what new opportunities it holds for your nonprofit.

- *Customers/target market.* Annual reports often illustrate how the company has served its customers. Study these examples to help you understand how the company adds value for its customers.

- *Challenges and problems.* Focus on any mention of current or future competition, industry or economic trends, or how the company's target market perceives its products and services. Presenting yourself as a problem solver gives your prospect one more good reason to buy from you.

19A.5   *Financial Statements*

In this section, pay closest attention to the company's income statement. To help you understand what you are reading and what the figures mean, remember (1) the numbers acquire meaning only in comparison with a company's past performance and to other companies in the industry, (2) percentages are more important than absolute numbers, and (3) numbers only offer clues as to a company's performance—they tell you the final score, but not how the game was played.

If contemplating your prospect's income statement leaves you wondering where to begin, follow this four-step plan:

1. *Analyze your prospect company's top line or total revenues.* Did sales increase or decrease and why? How did revenue growth compare to industry trends? Was growth attributable more to volume increases or price increases?

2. *Skip down to the bottom line.* Compare profit increases or decreases with revenue increases or decreases. How did profits compare to their peer group?

3. *Analyze the operating income figures.* Also shown as earnings before interest and taxes, these figures should appear several lines above the net income figure. Operating income numbers are the best measure of how well company managers run the company's day-to-day operations. These figures factor out decisions about company finances and taxes and extraordinary events, where your products will have no impact anyway.

4. *Take a look at gross profit margins.* A company's gross profits are a valuable measure of its effectiveness and ability to add value for its customers. Large revenue increases accompanied by lower gross profit margins, for example, may mean that the company can attract more business only through lower prices.

Since customers and prospects don't come with directions or an owner's manual explaining how to sell to them, why not take advantage of the next best thing? Competitive salespeople need to use all the resources at their disposal, and an annual report provides fast, easy access to valuable customer information.

It's impossible to know much about your prospects and customers. Annual reports are a gold mine of information and serve as a how-to guide for selling to any company that publishes one.

The following are three good reasons to make annual reports part of your selling strategy:

1. *To be more than just a vendor.* Professionals want salespeople to know their business and industry—their sources of competitive advantage, challenges, and opportunities—information you can find in many companies' annual reports.

2. *To earn the right to an appointment.* You can use the information in an annual report to demonstrate a thorough knowledge of your customer's business that will help you get an appointment. The annual report can also familiarize you with the customer-specific jargon, financial measurements, and current trends that will help you "speak the language" when you do get an appointment.

3. *To find out how you can help.* Consider a company's annual report the scorecard of its performance. Careful analysis can tell you how you and your nonprofit organization might be able to enhance that performance— ideas you can then present to your customer in a persuasive presentation.

The next section relates to one of the dominant trends in today's business world that is an asset for nonprofit organizations—cause-related marketing.

19A.6   *Cause-Related Marketing Is Good Business*

Cause-related marketing (CRM) is a growing trend as corporations are discovering that what's good for the community is also good for business. Cause-related marketing ties a company's charitable contributions to the sale of products and services in order to increase consumer awareness and company image.

Organized to increase the bottom line, business sponsorship has gone from approximately 1,000 companies spending $450 million in 1984 to 21,000+ companies spending $9.2 billion in 2001. In each instance, these sponsorships have required that there be a cause-related marketing component to the sponsorship. Cause-related marketing will continue to increase as more and more companies seek nontraditional methods of supporting products. Every company and nonprofit organization develops its own format for choosing and evaluating a CRM program, but the following gives some introductory guidelines and philosophies of both:

- *Good company citizenship is good business.* It has been proven time and again that those companies exhibiting conscience are consistently the most successful. The recent Cone/Roper Benchmark Survey found that 75 percent of all people questioned expressed the importance of buying from companies that make charitable contributions.
- *Check references.* Corporations and charities should check each other out with the same due diligence as hiring a new employee. Corporations need to analyze how a charity spends its money, and they should talk with other corporations who have worked with the charity to determine its credibility. Charities need to take the time to study a corporation to determine its reputation in the community.
- *Target audience.* A successful CRM campaign must match the cause to the desired target audience of a corporation. An alcohol company would typically not look towards a children's charity; obviously a tobacco company would not either.
- *Lead time.* One of the most important elements of a successful cause-related marketing program effort is lead time. Packaged goods manufacturers were some of the first to use CRM and have reaped the most benefits, in part because they have more time to work on a campaign than other corporations.
- *Timing.* The timing of the program itself is important. Companies often try cause-related marketing when sales are low. This type of approach almost always fails. The best programs should not be run in the best months or worst months for a company. Somewhere in-between is the best.
- *Involve employees.* The best CRM programs are team efforts that involve all levels of employees. When the chief executive officer (CEO) of a corporation stands shoulder-to-shoulder with employees in a program, it makes for a winner.
- *State your goals.* Don't just announce a cause-related tie-in. Say what it's for. The promotional message should state the amount of money trying to be raised, and what it will be used for. This will help people identify with and develop empathy for the cause.
- *Dominate a cause.* Corporations will see the most benefit if they can be the preeminent benefactor. If you are splitting your efforts among several charitable organizations, you tend to lose exposure.

Following are highlights from the Cone Roper Benchmark Study:

Increased Consumer Acceptance

- Americans are significantly more receptive to CRM than ever before. Seventy-six percent believe it's acceptable for companies to engage in CRM.
- Cynicism towards CRM is quite low. Only 21 percent of those surveyed questioned the motives of companies that help good causes.

- Receptivity to CRM is greatest among those most likely to make key purchasing decisions: women 18–49 (84 percent), parents of young children (81 percent), and influentials (81 percent).

Increased Impact

- When price and quality are equal, 76 percent of consumers would be more likely to switch to a brand associated with a good cause.
- When price and quality are equal, 76 percent of consumers would be likely to switch to a retail outlet associated with a good cause.

Issues Closest to Home Have Greatest Acceptance

- More than half of those surveyed (59 percent) want companies to get involved in improving the quality of life on their local level rather than at the national or global levels.
- Consumers believe companies should take greater steps to deal with the issues of crime (41 percent), the environment (35 percent), public education (35 percent), and poverty (24 percent). The 1999 Cone/Roper Trend Report indicates a waning interest in companies dealing with the issues of drug abuse, homelessness, and substances.

(A) METHODOLOGY

As defined by the 1999 Cone/Roper Report, CRM is a strategic marketing practice which links a company or its products to a social cause or issue. The goal of CRM is to create enduring bonds and lasting relationships with consumers, employees, retailers, distributors, customers, local communities, and key influencers, as well as to enhance brand equity and increased sales and differentiate parity products in a cluttered marketplace. The study continues to be the industry benchmark for CRM.

Cause-related marketing is here to stay. As with all marketing, the corporations that are successful with it will be the ones that take the time to understand it, evaluate it, and improve upon it. Unfortunately, like so many other marketing strategies, CRM has become a buzzword that many nonprofits and corporations toss around, but have no idea how to incorporate into their plans. A successful CRM program must create a win–win situation for both the corporation and the nonprofit.

The standard for a successful CRM program was set 19 years ago with the joint restoration committee for the Statue of Liberty. During a three-month period in 1983, American Express donated one cent for each transaction on its American Express Card. This program resulted in a $1.7 million donation to the restoration of the Statue of Liberty and increased the use of the card by over 20 percent. This is a classic example of a true win–win program.

Many nonprofits continue to view CRM as a simple donation to a charity without understanding that the corporation must benefit. Corporations have also tried to shy away from their responsibility by soliciting programs that use a charity's name but don't deliver solid financial rewards to the nonprofit.

Cause-related marketing is a tested winner and has earned exceptional marketing results for corporations, but, as with any strategy, it needs to be done with the right resources and the proper thought process.

When contacting corporations, be sure you know where to look for money.

19A.7 How to Work with Corporations: Marketing versus Philanthropy

According to the Internal Revenue Service, corporations may give up to 10 percent of their pretax income in tax-deductible donations. However, most large businesses give away only about 1 percent of their pretax dollars. Unless corporations have a separately endowed foundation, such as Prudential, giving is very closely tied to profits, and if a corporation does not make a profit one year, giving may drop sharply the next.

(A) THREE CORPORATE FUNDING DOORS

Unfortunately, the majority of nonprofits don't know how to ask corporations for money. They approach them in the same way they approach foundations and government, and this is a mistake. To raise money from a corporation, you need to think like one.

Think of a corporation as having three doors for nonprofits to enter when they seek assistance. The first door is called *membership.* This is a very small door around the side of the building where the corporation sets aside a small amount of money to join chambers of commerce, trade associations, and civic groups such as the Lions and Rotary. Corporate membership contributions are generally in the $100 to $500 range. If you have a membership program or can develop a corporate category within an overall donor program, this is a good way to get on the corporate radar screen.

The second door, toward the front of the building, is the *philanthropy* entrance. This is the traditional door used by the majority of nonprofit organizations. Corporate grants are usually in the $1,000 to $10,000 range and are given on a year-to-year basis. The corporate giving staff are frequently housed in the public relations department (a tip off to the next level of funding), and their goal is to spread the limited philanthropic dollars over a large number of organizations. Corporations like their employees to be involved in the giving process, and so a corporate person on your board or a committee can be instrumental in securing continued or long-term funding for your group.

If the corporation does not have a presence in your community, the chances of receiving support are minimal. However, although companies in your community are always the best bet, be on the lookout for corporations that will be moving to your area or that are planning to buy out an existing company. They want some quick visibility, and this is an excellent opportunity to get your organization's message across before they arrive; you must compete with all the other groups. The health care and banking industries are prime examples of a rapidly changing business climate where companies look to build a corporate identity and community acceptance as quickly as possible.

Don't forget that companies of all sizes are excellent places to obtain donated office equipment, food and supplies, volunteers, and technical experts. Small local businesses are often overlooked, but when every dollar counts explore your options for free food at board meetings, printing and copying, or flowers for your special event.

The third door, right at the front of the building, is the *marketing* entrance. Corporations spend billions of dollars every year to market their goods and services, and if your nonprofit can assist the company to enhance its image, reach potential customers, or reinforce existing customer relationships, they will want to work with you. Besides, it's good business for corporations to tax shelter their marketing dollars through your organization.

During the past decade, the majority of corporate dollars going to nonprofit groups have come from the marketing rather than philanthropic budgets. In CRM, the relationship moves from that of grantor–grantee to one of partnering in projects to benefit both the company and the nonprofit. Bill Shore, director of Share our Strength and author of *Revolution of the Heart,* was a leader in this technique in the 1980s with Charge Against Hunger, a partnership with American Express. Now we see it everywhere.

What are companies looking for? Usually, most companies want to promote the image of:

- A friendly and caring corporate citizen responding to critical community needs (Corporations are becoming heavily involved in high-risk youth and education issues.)
- A protector of the environment ("Dolphin-friendly" tuna and "save the rain forest" products are overflowing from supermarket shelves.)
- A company that treats its employees well (Day care and elder care concerns are moving to the top of many corporate agendas.)

What does it take for a nonprofit to raise money through CRM? A bit of chutzpah, a basic understanding of what the corporation and your nonprofit are looking for, some confidence, and a real desire to move the relationship into a true partnership. Put yourself inside the mind of the marketing director who is asking "What can this organization do for me?" If you can figure out a way to help the company get in front of customers while generating resources for your nonprofit, you have a win–win situation.

Can't think of where to start? Pull together a group of your stakeholders for a creative session, and let the ideas flow freely. Think of all the possible corporations within your area and all the possible projects you might work on together. Some ideas to get you started include the following:

- A publication or service that meets the needs of your constituents and the corporation's customers (A traffic safety group might obtain corporate sponsorship from an insurance company.)
- A needed service for the corporation's employees (A counseling center might negotiate an Employee Assistance Program contract to provide counseling services.)
- Help corporations to comply with the law (A disability group might market its "accessibility audit" services.)

- Get your message across to the public in a well-traveled corporate thoroughfare (An arts group might obtain sponsorship for a display in a corporate lobby. This works just as well for human service groups.)
- Persuade a supermarket to devote a certain percentage of its sales to your group on a given day (Increase sales by mobilizing your supporters to shop in that store.)

When you have lots of possibilities, you can begin to narrow the focus and pick one or two corporations to approach.

It is best to start with companies where you already have a relationship or where you have someone who can introduce you to a senior executive. Look to the bank where you have your account or the company where a number of your volunteers are employed. Sometimes you may decide to look at companies where you will become a customer. If you decide to shift your bank account, use the opportunity to negotiate for a new line of credit or a reduction in service charges.

When you have identified a likely prospect, find out everything you can about them. Request a copy of their annual report and corporate giving policies, review the information in the *New Jersey Grants Guide,* check out the corporation's Web page (if they have one), and talk with other people in the community who have had either philanthropic or business dealings with the company.

(B) DEVELOPING THE PARTNERSHIP

The next step is to call up the CEO, the marketing director, or any person in the company who is accessible to you and discuss the possibilities of developing a partnership. Remember that they are looking for visibility, credibility, and new customers. As an example, a bank may be interested in marketing its services to the African-American community in your neighborhood. You may have a small budget, but a lot of credibility with the people you serve. A fairly typical approach would be to ask the bank to sponsor a neighborhood fair.

This is a good start, but it provides a finite sum of money for your nonprofit and only superficial exposure for the bank. Why not offer to follow up the fair by working with the bank over the next year to develop other strategies and opportunities to market their services to your constituency (their potential customers). The difference here is the desire of the nonprofit organization to work with the bank throughout the year on a variety of approaches. In this way, you can educate the company on the needs of your community, they can develop products to suit your constituents, and your nonprofit develops a regular stream of income.

Are there risks in this approach? Sure there are. You would be foolish to think CRM is a free lunch. It is important to discuss prospective partnerships with your board of directors and other key stakeholders, particularly if you think the partnership might have any negative repercussions with your staff, immediate constituencies, or existing and future funders. Remember that the company will probably be much clearer about its self-interest than you will about yours. This is why it's good to have a few businesspeople on your board of directors to help you evaluate opportunities.

Bear in mind that corporations are one of the principal engines that drive our society. If we want to have long-term support from this funding source, we need to look inside the corporate mindset and ask ourselves how they can support our mission, while we help the business support theirs. In some cases, we just want to ask them to pay a membership fee; in others, we will want a straightforward donation; but for those who want to take the relationship into a partnership, the rewards (and also the risks) can be greater.

All the knowledge in the world won't make you a good salesperson. In the next section you will find techniques of good salespeople and traits of ineffective salespeople.

(C) HOW TO BE MORE EFFECTIVE AT STRATEGIC SELLING

Whether you need $5,000 or $5,000,000, you need to have sales training and experience. However, many nonprofits have never had formal training or experience selling anything. As a result, they make mistakes that alienate potential contributors and, ultimately, lose sales.

The protocol of selling is actually very easy to learn. By following a formula of 10 steps, you can increase your effectiveness as a salesperson and generate more revenue than you ever thought possible.

Step 1. Be goal oriented. In sales, as in any aspect of business, it is critical to be goal oriented. If you don't have specific goals, you will not be able to measure your progress effectively and examine what you need to do to become better at your job. In order to set realistic goals, look at your revenue over the past two years. Has there been a steady rate of growth? Do you anticipate any activity that will impact your sales positively or negatively over the next year? Determine what level you need to reach in order to be successful. Remember that your goals have to be reasonable. Unless there are extremely extenuating circumstances, you cannot expect to increase your sales by 200 percent in one year. A more realistic goal would be 10 to 30 percent.

Step 2. Write your goals down. After you have taken the time and effort to set your goals, write them down. If you think you can skip that step, you are wrong. Goals that are not written down are just dreams. Turn your dreams into reality by picking up your pen. When not written down, goals become cloudy and may hinder the success of your plan. Writing your goals down is a great way to refresh your memory and keep you focused.

Step 3. Know your product. It is amazing how many people walk into a prospect's office without a thorough knowledge of the products or services they provide. Without such knowledge, there is no way to identify how you can fill the client's needs. Do your homework *before* you meet with a potential client. (Remember the annual report?) Know what benefits and rights you can—and cannot—provide. This way, you have all of the information you need to make an effective presentation, and your client will appreciate your respect for his or her time.

Step 4. Identify the client's needs. The most effective salespeople see themselves as problem solvers, identifying the barriers that their customers are facing and providing the tools to break down those barriers. Put yourself in your prospect's shoes and try to determine how you can best help your prospect accomplish his or her goals. Present your opportunity with a benefits orientation. Make sure the prospect understands the benefits. Once they do, the prospect becomes a donor.

Step 5. Never, never lie. While pointing out benefits and offering additional benefits is important, it is even more important not to mislead the client in your presentation. Promising more than you can deliver is the quickest way to lose credibility and clients. If the prospect asks you something about which you are unsure, tell the prospect, "That's a good question. Let me get back to you on that." If the prospect asks you for something you know you cannot deliver, be honest and say so. Then see if you can help the prospect resolve the situation in some other way.

Step 6. Pay attention to the details. From maintaining a neat appearance to checking proposals for typographical errors, it is important to pay attention to the impression you are making. Once you make the sale, be sure that the product gets delivered or the client gets regular updates on the service. Attention to detail builds strong relationships and repeat sales.

Step 7. Follow through. At each point in the sales process, it is important to follow through to the next level. From calling on a hot lead to making sure that your proposal was received, not following through in sales is the equivalent of dropping the ball in a football game. Failure to follow through shows a lack of commitment and makes a bad impression on would-be clients.

Step 8. Be tenacious. Anyone who has been in sales for any length of time knows that getting a "yes" to a sales pitch on the first visit or through the first contact is a rare occurrence. Often, it takes a sales representative several contacts and repeated follow-through to prove him or herself to a client. Estimates are that 90 percent of salespeople give up too soon. By being tenacious, continuing to provide the client with information, and offering your services, you can ultimately reach the proper intersection of timing, need, and action.

Step 9. Know when to close and when to walk away. You have followed all of the steps and have a prospect that seems very interested. Now is the time to ask for the order. There are many different ways to do this, and you will have to determine which is right for you. Unfortunately, in spite of your best efforts to be prepared, identify your client's needs, create a good impression, and follow through diligently, there will be prospects that will not initially say "yes." There comes a point in the sales process where, if the prospect becomes unreasonable or if you have come to an impasse, you need to walk away. Recognizing when you are wasting your time on a prospect with irrational demands or a budget that is too small is just as important as knowing when to close.

Step 10. Get to work. Once the sale is complete, you have only done 10 percent of the work. You must now ensure the best possible service. Keep in contact with your donors to stay on top of their progress. If there are any problems, handle them in a timely, professional manner. Make your donor feel as if he or she is your top priority. Follow through with all promised benefits, and you can be assured of renewals.

19A.8   Shared Qualities of Top Sellers

The Harvard Business School did a study to determine the common characteristics of top salespeople. The evidence they found is clear that most people can be top sellers if they are willing to study, concentrate, and focus on their performance. Here are the attributes the study found in highly successful salespeople:

- *Did not take "no" personally and allow it to make them feel like a failure.* They have high enough levels of confidence or self-esteem so that, although they may be disappointed, they are not devastated.

- *100 percent acceptance of responsibility for results.* They didn't blame the economy, the competition, or their company for dips in closings. Instead, the worse things were, the harder they worked to make negatives work to their advantage.
- *Above average ambition and desire to succeed.* This is a key area because it affected priorities and how they spent their time on and off the job, with whom they associated, and so on.
- *High levels of empathy.* The ability to put themselves in the customer's shoes, imagine needs and concerns, and respond appropriately was a habit.
- *Intensely goal oriented.* Always knowing what they were going after and how much progress they were making kept distractions from side-tracking them.
- *Above-average willpower and determination.* No matter how tempted they were to give up, they persisted toward goals. Self-discipline was a key.
- *Impeccably hones with self and the customer.* No matter what the temptation to fudge, these people resisted and gained ongoing trust of customers.
- *Ability to approach strangers even when it is uncomfortable.*

How many did you rate high in? What should you be doing to help yourself? Selling is a great field filled with opportunity. But that opportunity must be utilized, and that takes concentration and focus. The S-Myth (that's sales myth)—salespeople are born, not made, debunked again!

19A.9   Rules for Success

Much of selling is self-motivated and self-driven. Following are 10 rules for success as a salesperson:

1. Believe that you have already succeeded before you even begin the task. Act, dress, and speak not for who you are now but for who you want to be.
2. Replace negative statements with positive phrases. Tell yourself "I am a good person." "I am a success." Practice this before going to bed and upon waking in the morning.
3. Take responsibility for your actions and your life. Never allow yourself to blame others for your lack of success. Even though an event might be caused by someone else and is out of your control, control your own reaction to the event.
4. Think positively about all of your accomplishments, no matter how small they may appear to others. They are your building blocks of success.
5. Formulate a mission statement and keep it with you at all times.
6. Remind yourself of great success stories and the difficulties those people had in accomplishing their goals. Such examples as Helen Keller and Winston Churchill remind us that our problems and tribulations are small fish in a great sea.
7. When taking on a new project, ask yourself: "What is the worst that can happen?"

8. Allow yourself to make mistakes. It is an essential growth component.

9. Strive to be the best you can, not the best there is. You may find, however, that one leads to the other.

10. No one was born a great doctor, lawyer, or salesperson. We all came into the world as babies. We all become what we are based on the choices we make. You can choose success.

19A.10   Common Enemies of Salespeople

The better we are at defeating the common enemies that all salespeople face, the more successful we will be. These enemies are as follows:

- *Ego.* Our egos make us think that what we have to say is more important than what the customer has to say, so we memorize product knowledge and dump data on any prospect that will stand still long enough to listen.

- *Too much talk.* Because what we have to say is all important, we pitch customers. The best salespeople know that the pay in selling is far greater for asking the right questions than for knowing the right answers. I have yet to hear of a salesperson listening himself out of a deal.

- *Poor listening habits.* Because we talk too much, we listen poorly. If you truly want to listen better, don't talk. Nature abhors a vacuum and someone's words will rush in to fill the void. If they are not yours, they will be those of the customer. The person who talks will monopolize the conversation, while the person who listens will control the conversation.

- *Assumptions about what's on the customer's mind.* Because we have been listening poorly, we think we know what the customer should want, rather than what she does want.

- *Talking about things that don't interest the customer.* A carefully constructed, canned pitch will normally contain something like 20 feature benefits, and the salesperson will tell the customer all about every one of them. This dumps the whole load on the customer, but customers buy for their reasons, not ours. Customers will usually have only one or two primary buying motives. Talking about other things only distracts, confuses, and bores the customer.

- *Failing to determine the customer's attitude.* A customer can have only one of three attitudes at any given time: acceptance, objection, or indifference. If we know how to determine the customer's attitude accurately, and how to respond appropriately, we will be well on the way to a sale.

- *Not asking for the order.* Our fragile egos tell us that if the customer rejects the offer, it is really a personal rejection. We feel slighted and fail to ask for a commitment of any kind. If you ask, you get. The more you ask, the more you get. If you don't ask, you don't get. It's just that simple.

- *Lack of well-defined goals and objectives.* If you don't know where you are going, how will you know when you have arrived?

- *Not taking notes.* If we don't write down what is important to the customer, we will forget and talk about what we think is important. The strongest memory is weaker than the palest ink.

19A.11 Characteristics of Good Salespeople

The two basic qualities that good salespeople must have are empathy and ego drive.

- *Empathy,* the important central ability to *feel* as the other person does in order to be able to sell a product or service, must be possessed in large measure. Having empathy does not necessarily mean being sympathetic. One can know what the other fellow feels without agreeing with that feeling. Salespeople simply cannot sell well without the invaluable and irreplaceable ability to get powerful feedback from the potential sponsor through empathy.
- *Ego drive; Need to conquer.* The second of the basic qualities absolutely needed by good salespeople is a particular kind of ego drive which makes them want and need to make the sale in a personal or ego way, not merely for the money to be gained. The feeling must be that the sale must be made; the customers are there to help salespeople fulfill their personal need. In effect, to top salespeople, the sale—the conquest—provides a power means of enhancing the ego. Their self-picture improves dramatically by virtue of conquest, and diminishes with failure.

Because of the nature of all selling, salespeople will fail to sell more often than they will succeed. Thus, since failure tends to diminish their self-picture, their ego cannot be so weak that the poor self-picture continues for too long a time. Rather, the failure must act as a trigger—as a motivation toward greater efforts—that with success will bring the ego enhancements needed. A subtle balance must be found between an ego partially weakened in precisely the right way to need a great deal of enhancement (the sale) and an ego sufficiently strong to be motivated by failure but not shattered by it.

The salesperson's empathy, coupled with his or her intense ego drive, enables him or her to hone in on the target effectively and make the sale. Salespeople have the drive—the need to make the sale—and empathy gives them the connecting tool with which to do it.

(A) SYNERGISTIC EFFECTS

People with a strong ego drive have maximum motivation to fully capitalize on whatever empathy they possess. Needing the sale, they are not likely to let their empathy spill over and become sympathy. Their ego need for the conquest is not likely to allow them to side with the customer; rather, it spurs them on to use their knowledge of the customer fully to make the sale.

On the other hand, salespeople with little or no ego drive are hardly likely to use their empathy in a persuasive manner. They understand people and may know perfectly well what things to say to close the sale effectively, but their understanding is apt to become sympathy. If they do not need the conquest, their very knowledge of the real needs of the potential customer may tell them that the customer, in fact, should not buy. Since they do not need the sale in an *inner* personal sense, they may not persuade the customer to buy.

Thus, there is a dynamic relationship between empathy and ego drive. It takes a combination of the two, each working to reinforce the other—each enabling the other to be fully utilized—to make the successful salesperson. Keeping these two aspects in balance—empathy and ego drive—will help you be more successful in your sponsorship solicitations.

Once you have an understanding of empathy and ego drive, your next step is to understand the psychology of selling. But, first, ask yourself the following six questions:

1. Am I proud to be a salesperson?
2. Am I in the top 20 percent of salespeople?
3. Do I genuinely like myself?
4. Is there any aspect of selling that makes me uncomfortable?
5. Does my self-concept include a high level of income?
6. Can I cope with the rejection that I will inevitably encounter in selling?

The most important thing you have to understand in the world of selling is that nothing happens until the sale takes place, and, in selling, the 80–20 rule, or the Pareto principle, prevails. According to the 80–20 rule, 80 percent of sales are made by 20 percent of the salespeople, and once you get into the top 20 percent, you don't have to worry about money or employment again.

Selling is an inner game. That is, what is going on inside the mind of the salesperson makes all the difference to his or her success. We know there is a direct relationship between a salesperson's self-concept and his or her sales performance and effectiveness. You will feel uncomfortable if you don't act in accordance with your self-concept, and you will always sell in a manner consistent with your self-concept. Some of us are uneasy about picking up the telephone and calling somebody: others of us are uncomfortable about closing. By becoming more skilled, we feel more competent, raise our self-concept, and become more successful.

The core of self-concept is self-esteem. People with high self-esteem like themselves. How much you like yourself is the key determinant of your performance and your effectiveness in everything you do.

There are two major obstacles in selling. The first obstacle is the customer's fear of making a mistake. The second major obstacle in selling is the salesperson's fear of rejection. Until a salesperson develops confidence, a high self-concept, and sufficient resilience to bounce back from inevitable rejection, they cannot sell successfully. All outstanding salespeople have reached the point where they no longer fear rejection.

Sales are usually based on friendship. People will not buy from you until they are genuinely convinced that you are their friend and are acting in their best interest. There is a direct relationship between your level of self-esteem and how well you get along with different people. The best salespeople have a natural ability to make friends easily with prospective customers.

A key element in selling is enthusiasm and a passion for what you are doing. A sale is a transfer of your enthusiasm and passion about your sponsorship opportunity into the mind and heart of the other person.

The reason so many people fail in sales is that they do not stay with it long enough to get those first few winning experiences that raise their self-esteem and

self-concept and set them off on a successful career in selling. That's why it's so important that, from the very beginning, you say to yourself that nothing is going to stop you until you are successful.

19A.12   Summary

Ego, empathy, self-esteem, confidence, enthusiasm, determination, follow-through, listening skills, understanding the donor, attention to detail, understanding of CRM, and understanding your product are all necessary to becoming a successful salesperson. Start developing these traits, and watch your success!

Evolutionary Environment

LEADERSHIP

HUMAN RESOURCE DEVELOPMENT
AND MANAGEMENT

Organizational Culture and Nonprofit Organizations[1] (New)

Joseph E. Champoux, PhD
The Robert O. Anderson Schools of Management
The University of New Mexico

27A.1 Introduction

Organizational culture is a complex and deep aspect of organizations that can strongly affect organization members. Organizational culture includes the values, norms, rites, rituals, ceremonies, heroes, and scoundrels in the organization's history. It defines the content of what a new employee needs to learn to be accepted as a member of the organization.

Key aspects of organizational culture include a sharing of values and a structuring of organizational experiences. Different sets of values can coexist among different groups of people throughout an organization. Although values differ from group to group, members of each group can share a set of values. Not all people in an organization will fully agree about the dominant values and norms.

If you have traveled abroad, you have already experienced what it is like to enter a new, different, and "foreign" culture. The architecture you saw was different from that at home. The food was not what you commonly ate. The language may have been different, possibly causing you some difficulty in communication. People in the new culture behaved differently toward each other than you were accustomed to behaving. You probably felt some anxiety about learning your way around the new culture so you would not stand out as a "foreigner." Organizational cultures are similar to cultures of different countries. Your entry into a new organizational culture will have many features of entering the culture of another country.

All human systems that have endured for sometime, and whose members have a shared history, develop a culture. The specific content of an organization's culture develops from the experiences of a group adapting to its external environment and building a system of internal coordination. Each human system within which you interact has a culture. Your family, your college or university, your employer, and any leisure time organizations such as sororities, fraternities, or cultural organizations all have their own cultures. These cultures can make different—and sometimes conflicting—demands on you.

Organizational cultures divide into multiple subcultures. An organization's design creates varying substructures and processes within the organization. Subcultures grow readily within these differentiated parts of the total organization. They also grow readily within departments, divisions, and different operating locations of an organization.

Different occupational groups within an organization often form different subcultures. Specialists in art displays, accounting, information systems, and fund raising often have their own jargon that helps them talk to each other. That jargon becomes an integral part of an occupational subculture and often cannot be understood by those outside the subculture. An information systems specialist easily understands terms like *upload, download,* and *token ring networks,* which often are a foreign language to people outside that occupation.

Workforce diversity and the global environment of organizations, discussed in "Welcoming Differences: Diversity and the Not-for-Profit Organization." Elizabeth Power in *Nonprofit Handbook,* Second Edition, 1998 Supplement, p. 138, also help build subcultures in organizations. People from different social backgrounds and who have different values will infuse organizations with a variety of values and viewpoints. Global operations often require organizations to hire people from the host country. Those employees often will bring values into the organization that differ from those of the organization's home country.

27A.2   *Levels of Organizational Culture*

Organizational cultures are revealed to us at three different but related levels: artifacts, values, and basic assumptions. These levels vary in their visibility to an outsider. The first is the easiest to see and the last is the most difficult. Exhibit 27A.1 shows the three levels of organizational culture and their visibility to an outsider.

Artifacts are the most visible parts of an organization's culture. They are the obvious features of an organization that are immediately visible to a new employee. Artifacts include sounds, architecture, smells, behavior, attire, language, products, and ceremonies.

Organizations differ in the layout of their interior space and the formality of their working relationships. Do people work in an open office space or behind closed doors? Do people dress formally or informally? Does the interior design give the impression of a cheerful or a somber work environment? Do people refer

EXHIBIT 27A.1 Organizational Culture Diagnosis Worksheet

Visible Artifacts

I. Physical Characteristics
(Architecture, Office Layout, Decor, Attire)

II. Behavior (Interpersonal and Oral)
(Language, Interpersonal Orientation, Use of Titles, Rites,
Rituals, Stories, Anecdotes, Heroines, Heroes)

III. Public Documents
(Annual Reports, Press Accounts, Web Sites,
Internal Newspapers, Newsletters)

Invisible Artifacts

IV. Values
(Espoused Values, In-Use Values)

V. Basic Assumptions
(Aspects of Behavior, Perceptions of Internal
and External Relationships, Thoughts, Feelings)

Source: Suggested by the analysis in E. H. Schein. (1992). *Organizational Culture and Leadership,* 2nd ed. San Francisco: Jossey-Bass Publishers, Part One; T. E. Deal, and A. A. Kennedy. (1982). *Corporate Cultures.* Reading, MA: Addison-Wesley, Chapter 7.

to each other by first names or do they use formal titles such as Doctor, Mr., Ms., and Lieutenant? These factors are clues to an organization's culture. You can infer some values, norms, and required behavior from such factors. A new employee must first attend to messages from the physical characteristics of the organization and then watch the behavior of veteran organization members.

At the next level of awareness are the values embedded in the culture. Values tell organization members what they *ought* to do in various situations. Values are hard for the newcomer to see, but she can discover and learn them. The newcomer must be wary of espoused values that guide what veteran members say in a given situation. More important are the in-use values that guide the behavior of organization members.[2] For example, a new employee learns from talking to superiors that equal promotion opportunity for women and men is the organization's policy. The person then finds that only men were promoted to management positions in the last five years.

The last level of discovery is almost invisible to a new employee. Even veteran organization members are not consciously aware of the basic assumptions of the organization's culture. Like values, these assumptions guide behavior in organizations. As a culture matures, many values become basic assumptions. Basic assumptions deal with many aspects of human behavior, human relationships within the organization, and relationships with elements in the organization's external environment. These assumptions develop over the history of the organization and from its ways of dealing with various events.

Because the assumptions are unconscious, veteran members find it hard to describe them to a new employee. People learn about them from trial-and-error behavior and by watching how veteran employees behave in different situations.

27A.3   *Cultural Symbolism*

Cultural symbolism is a perspective on organizational culture that lets you view a culture as a system of symbols that have meaning only to members of that culture. Some aspects of cultural symbolism may have meaning for a wide group of members while other aspects are significant for only a small number of employees. This view of organizational cultures looks at artifacts as described earlier, but also examines anything within the culture that has symbolic meaning to its members.

Cultural symbols have several characteristics. They represent more than the symbol alone by capturing emotional, cognitive, ethical, and aesthetic meanings. Symbols efficiently summarize those meanings for organization members. They serve the important cultural function of bringing order to otherwise complex events and processes, especially those that are repeated.

Symbols can be action symbols, verbal symbols, or material symbols. *Action symbols* are sets of behaviors that have meaning beyond the obvious aspects of the behavior. *Verbal symbols* are the stories, slogans, sagas, legends, and jargon that both distinguish people in a culture and carry special meanings for them. *Material symbols* are found in the physical features of an organization's culture, including architecture, interior decor, and types of clothing.

Symbols vary in complexity. They can be as simple as Xerox Corporation's slogan of "Leadership through Quality," a verbal symbol used in the 1980s to emphasize the company's program of continuous quality improvement and efforts to regain market share in copiers. Symbols can also be more complex such as regularly scheduled meetings where people decide matters but also define the organization's values and priorities in decision making.

Some research says symbols and espoused values should be congruent. For example, an organization that says it accepts or values diversity should also provide vegetarian dishes in the company's cafeteria for its vegetarian employees. Other research says you will find differences between espoused values and related symbols. An espoused value of equal status among employees may clash with the material symbols of larger offices for higher-status employees. That inconsistency gives you other information about the organization's culture—its lingering conflict between desires for equality and desires for status differences.

A third line of research offers the most complex view of cultural symbols. It suggests that you examine the meanings of espoused values and cultural symbols for what they say and what they do not say. An analysis of a verbal symbol such as a story would look for puns, metaphors, unstated assumptions, and what was not said along with what was said.

As an example of how one gets different information by looking at symbols from different perspectives, consider the following story told publicly by a company president.

> We have a young woman who is extraordinarily important to the launching of a major new (product). We will be talking about it next Tuesday in its first worldwide introduction. She arranged to have her Caesarean yesterday in order to be prepared for this event. We have insisted that she stay home and that this be televised via closed circuit television, so we're having this done by TV for her, and she is staying home three months and we are finding ways of filling in.[3]

The company president felt he had described deep company feeling and caring for the pregnant woman. He viewed the commitment of the television resources as an important symbol of the company's commitment to its employees. Further analysis suggests other meanings. Perhaps the company was putting the product introduction ahead of the woman's and the baby's needs. Saying "We have a young woman" could imply strong company control, an implicit assumption of the president.

27A.4   Functions of Organizational Culture

Organizational cultures can have many functional effects on organizations and their management. The two major areas to which they contribute are (1) adaptation to the organization's external environment and (2) coordination of internal systems and processes.

An organization that has adapted successfully to its external environment can develop a culture with a consensus among members about the organization's mission. Specific goals derived from the mission and the means to reach those goals will be part of the culture. A consensus about a mission among veteran members lets the organization move forward smoothly toward those goals. Members agree about what needs to be done and how it will be done. In short, an organization's culture can help its members develop a sense of identity with the organization and a clear vision of the organization's direction.

An organizational culture that gives its members a clear vision of the organization's mission also presents a consistent image to its markets, customers, and clients. Over time, that image can give an organization a competitive advantage by building commitment to its products or services.

Peter Drucker's analysis of high-performing nonprofit organizations shows cultures with a mission focus, a client focus, and self-motivated volunteers. A mission focus gives people in the organization a clear sense of direction and reason for being. A strong client focus keeps the nonprofit organization focused on client needs. Both foci can remind members of the organization of the need to constantly improve what they offer to their environment. Self-motivated volunteers are a key way in which nonprofit organizations attain their mission.

Members of developed organizational cultures agree about how to measure results and what remedial action to take if something goes wrong. Veteran members know almost automatically when things are not going right and how to take corrective action. If there were no consensus about those matters, conflict levels could be dysfunctionally high. With so much conflict among its members, the organization would have difficulty responding rapidly in situations requiring fast action.

Organizational cultures define the rewards and sanctions that managers can use. Rules develop about rewards for good performance and about sanctions for poor performance. Some cultures respond to poor performance by saying the individual is not properly matched to the task. Those organizations reassign the person to a new task and let him try again. Other cultures develop specific sanctions that include demotions and terminations.

Organizational cultures differ in the way they use reward systems. Some reward systems emphasize total organization performance, leading to a feeling that members are part of a fraternal group. Other cultures reward individual performance, ignoring the larger system. Members of the latter cultures develop a strong sense of individuality and independence.

Culture also helps integrate an organization's subsystems and processes. The integration lets the organization coordinate its various actions effectively. Common language develops within a culture, helping communication. Conceptual categories develop that filter unimportant detail and focus attention on important matters. Perceptual filtration reduces the likelihood that an individual will become overloaded by stimuli defined as unimportant by the culture.

The culture defines boundaries of groups and criteria for inclusion in the group. Well-defined group boundaries enhance member identification with the group and the group's work. Strong groups support and help members get their work done.

Organizational cultures define rules for power, rules for social stratification, and the ways social status is determined. Some accord social status and power to people of high achievement. Others base status and power on seniority.

The nature and quality of peer relationships and interpersonal interactions are defined by the organization's culture. Are interactions characterized by cooperation among peers at any cost or by confrontation and debate?

The last organizational culture function is the development and communication of an ideology of what the organization is all about. An ideology is a set of overarching values that collect all the basic assumptions embedded in the organization's culture. The ideology appears in stories about past successes or descriptions of organization heroes. The heroes may still be with the organization or may have left it long ago or passed on. In either case, what each hero represents stays in the ideology and becomes part of the organization's folklore. The ideology is a strong and sometimes overwhelming guide to action. As such, the ideology is an important element of an organization's culture that must be communicated to and discovered by the newcomer.

All the functions of organizational culture come together to serve an overarching function—reduction of anxiety and uncertainty in human relationships. Rules of conduct and ways of viewing the world outside and inside the organization let members distinguish important stimuli from unimportant. Ignoring some stimuli reduces the chance of overloading the human organism.

27A.5 *Dysfunctions of Organizational Culture*

The same functional features of an organization's culture can create dysfunctions. The last paragraph of the preceding section has the clues.

Changes in an organization's external environment often require changes in an organization's strategy. The existing organizational culture, though, has developed from a particular strategy, and members of the organization who are accustomed to that culture may resist changing the strategy. They may feel that such change will require changes in existing values and basic assumptions. When considering a change in strategy, managers must either dramatically change the existing culture or learn how to manage within its constraints.

The existing organizational culture can lead to dysfunctional results when the organization tries client, product, or market diversification, acquires another organization, or merges with another organization. Analyses of these changes ordinarily include financial, physical, and technical aspects of the proposed action, but rarely consider the culture of the target organization. A merger may result in merging incompatible cultures producing conflicts and inefficiencies. Moving into new markets brings the organization into new subcultures that may not respond in the usual ways to its product or service.

Organizations that introduce technologies to gain efficiency in providing service often experience latent dysfunctions. New technology can change familiar ways of acting that have become an accepted part of the existing organizational culture. Power and status may shift to those who know, understand, and use the new technology. Such shifts undermine the position of those who had power and status in the culture before the new technology arrived. All those factors can lead to conflict, inefficiency, and possible sabotage of the new technology.

Cultures produce different ways of looking at the world and interpreting language and events. People from different subcultures may distrust those from other subcultures because of their different worldviews. Conflict can erupt between people from different subcultures, especially when they passionately hold to different views.

Cultural differences can lead to communication failures between individuals even when they are expressing their thoughts clearly. For example, consider what the following words mean to you:

Tonic Braces Bubbler Ladder

Tonic is a soft drink in Boston, braces are suspenders in London, and a bubbler is a water fountain in Milwaukee. You might have trouble communicating with people in those cities if you do not know the meaning of those words.

Individuals from different subcultures within an organization have similar problems in communication. *Ladder,* for example, is printer's jargon for the arrangement of the same words in successive lines at the edges of a paragraph. People in the accounting department might not know that meaning of the word.

27A.6   *Diagnosing Organizational Culture*

Organizational culture diagnosis systematically assesses an organization's culture. You can diagnose a culture from two perspectives: (1) as an outsider considering a job with a certain organization, and (2) as an insider after you have joined an organization. Exhibit 27A.1 shows an Organizational Culture Diagnosis Worksheet that you can use to guide a diagnosis.

San Francisco's Shanti Project assessed their organization culture to prepare for a change in their increasingly diverse clients' needs. They had started as an organization that offered a range of services for the terminally ill. In the mid-1980s, a growing number of people with acquired immune deficiency syndrome (AIDS) had no source of reliable help, particularly emotional support. The Shanti Project's focus became their Emotional Support Program for people with AIDS and their loved ones. Their culture assessment uncovered an ever-present physical symbol— a box of tissues. Emotional comfort, symbolized by the box of tissues, had become the most important way Shanti served its changing client base.

(A) AS AN OUTSIDER

Diagnosing an organization's culture as a potential employee can help you decide whether that organization is where you can do well, thrive, and grow or whether the culture will make demands on you that you are unwilling or unable to meet. Although you will not learn all the inner secrets of a culture you have not yet joined, you can find clues about what it would be like to work for that organization.

Study the physical characteristics of the organization. What does the external architecture look like? Does it convey an image of a robust, durable, dependable organization? Does it convey a sense of indifference in the public statements the organization makes? Are the buildings the same quality for all employees, or are modern buildings reserved for senior executives? Visits to the headquarters or other work sites of an organization can give you valuable insights. Short of a physical visit, photographs in annual reports or press accounts are good approximations.

Read about the organization. Examine annual reports, press accounts about the organization, and its Web site. What do they describe? Do the reports emphasize the people who work for the organization and what they do or the financial performance of the organization? Each emphasis reflects a different culture. The first cares about the people who make up the organization. The second may care only about the *bottom line.* The choice is yours. Which culture do you prefer?

If you visit the organization as part of a recruiting interview, note how you are treated. You are an outsider. Are you treated as one or are you treated as a person about whom the organization cares?

Finally, talk to people who already work for the organization. Ask about the history of the organization, the criteria of success, and what it is like to work there every day.

You can develop many clues about an organization's culture by following these suggestions. Only an insider, however, can get to the inner secrets of the culture.

(B) AS AN INSIDER

After you join an organization, you can begin to dig deeper into its culture. Stories and anecdotes are a strong source of evidence about the important qualities of the culture. Watch for similarities among stories told by different people. The subjects emphasized in recurring stories are what is important to the organization's culture. They may include satisfied customers, getting ahead on your merits, or the politics of the organization. Stories often describe organization heroes. What did those heroes do? Pay close attention because a hero's actions likely imply important values in the organization's culture.

Find out the basis of promotions and pay increases. Are promotions based on competence and accomplishment or on tenure and loyalty to the organization? Such differences are clues to different types of organizational culture.

Observations of meetings are also useful sources of information about an organization's culture. Who does the talking? To whom do they talk? Such observations will tell you much about the status structure of the organization. Do participants defer to those with higher status or are all considered equal contributors?

What is the focus of meetings? How much time is spent on various topics? The topics discussed repeatedly and at length are clues about the culture's important values.

27A.7 Organizational Culture and Organizational Performance

Several lines of theoretical and empirical research point to a relationship between characteristics of an organization's culture and organizational performance. The theories vary in their explanations but all point to a link between culture and performance.

One theory says organizations have a competitive advantage when their culture is valuable, rare, and not easily imitated. The value of an organization's culture derives from the guidance it gives to direct people's behavior toward higher performance. Rarity refers to the features of a culture that are not common among competing organizations. Such rarity can come from the unique personalities of the organization's founders and the unique history underlying the culture. Cultures that are not easily imitated make it hard for competitors to change their cultures to get the same advantages. Difficulty of imitation follows partly from the rare features of some cultures and the basic difficulties confronting managers when trying to change a culture.

A second theoretical view focuses on environment-culture congruence. Organizations facing high complexity and high ambiguity require a cohesive culture for effective performance. They feature widely shared values and basic assumptions that guide people's behavior. For organizations facing low uncertainty and low complexity, building a cohesive culture could be costly. Those organizations will reach high performance with more formal control processes such as organization policies, rules, and procedures.

A third theory describes organizational cultures as having four distinct traits: involvement, consistency, adaptability, and mission. Involvement is the degree of employee participation in organizational decisions. The increased participation can increase employees' feelings of ownership in the organization. Consistency is the degree of agreement among organization members about important values and basic assumptions. Adaptability is the ability of the organization to respond to external changes with internal changes. Mission describes the core purposes of the organization that keep members focused on what is important to the organization. Empirical research found that involvement and adaptability were related to organizational growth. The consistency and mission traits were related to profitability. Empirical research is beginning to show a clear culture-performance link, though there are different theoretical explanations.

27A.8 Creating, Maintaining, and Changing Organizational Culture

Managers of modern organizations face three decisions about their organization's culture. They can decide to create a completely new culture, usually in a separate work unit or in a new organization. They can maintain their existing organizational culture because they believe it is right for their environment. They can decide to change their culture to a new set of values, basic assumptions, and ideologies.

Creating organizational culture is a deliberate effort to build a specific type of organizational culture. It happens when a founder forms a nonprofit organization to pursue a vision or when managers of an existing organization form a new operating unit. The new culture needs an ideology that is understandable, convincing, and widely discussed. The ideology is a key tool for getting organizational members to the vision.

Building the culture around that ideology is easier if managers can recruit and select people who already share key parts of the ideology or who can easily develop commitment to it. Formal socialization practices play major roles in building an identity with the ideology. Forging that identity is easier when people's values on entry are close to the values and beliefs of the ideology. Cultural symbols must also be consistent with the ideology. For example, if the ideology has egalitarian values, the organization should have few physical status symbols distinguishing senior managers from other employees.

Maintaining organizational culture does not mean that managers passively and uncritically accept the values and basic assumptions of the present culture. Maintenance of a culture presents managers with a dilemma. They want to hold on to the values that were successful in the past, but they also need to question whether those values are right for the organization's environment.

Culture maintenance requires managers to be aware of what organizational culture is and how it manifests itself in their organization. It requires knowing the existing organizational culture's artifacts, values, and ideologies. A key way managers can become familiar with their culture is by doing a culture diagnosis, as described earlier.

By maintaining their culture, managers want to maintain commitment of organization members to key parts of that culture. They also want to strengthen key values so they are widely held throughout the organization. In short, managers want to hold on to the good part of the organization's culture while helping the organization adapt to its newest challenges.

Culture maintenance requires managers to carefully examine any new practices for consistency with their culture's ideology. Introducing drug testing for employment screening in an organization with a culture built on trust might be a contradiction. Such testing might not appear contradictory in an organization that strongly values safety when working in hazardous areas.

Changing organizational culture requires breaking from some features of the old culture and creating new features. The size and depth of the change varies depending on the degree of difference between the desired new culture and the old. For example, changing the culture of an organization that has a homogeneous workforce to one that values diversity will require an extended effort. The change will reach deep into the cultural fabric of the organization over many years.

Successfully managing the change process requires managers to attend to several issues. One is choosing the correct time for change. They are advised to act when the times seem right for culture change or when the situation clearly demands it. An opportune time for culture change might be when the organization wishes to pursue favorable new markets. Change also might be required when the organization is performing poorly and faces clear threats to its viability.

Managers should not assume that everyone in the organization will share their view of the need to change. The senior executives of the organization will need to play leadership roles, convincing others in the organization that a culture change is needed by offering a vision of that new culture. Managers will need to move forward with confidence, persistence, and optimism about the new culture. The change effort can focus on many aspects of the organization's culture, such as ideology, values, and symbols, although it is not realistic to expect that all elements of the prior culture will be removed. Managers should know the roots of their organization's culture and maintain some continuity with the past by keeping elements that are valued widely in the organization.

27A.9   Institutionalizing a New Organizational Culture[4]

Institutionalization is the process that sustains changes in an organization over time. For nonprofit organizations, it means moving your organization to a new position and then holding it in that position. Holding does not mean fixed. It means sustaining or deepening the vision of the organization. Institutionalization also includes socialization processes needed to teach successive generations of members of the organization about the new vision.

Institutionalized behavior has three characteristics. It is persistent behavior, shared by two or more people in reaction to the same event, that is part of the cultural fabric of the organization. The latter is clearly the result wanted by those trying to change their organizational culture. They want those changes to be lasting events.

The institutionalization process follows three phases. During the *acquisition phase,* people learn the desired new behavior. This is the phase largely targeted by the cultural change efforts described above. The *reinforcement phase* shapes the desired behavior into its final and enduring forms. Managers rely heavily on the organization's reward system for the motivational tools that let them shape behavior. Because nonprofit organizations often pay lower salaries and benefits than many private-sector organizations, their managers must use rewards creatively. The last phase, the *transmission phase,* is important for the long-term retention of the new behaviors. It socializes newcomers to the behaviors needed by the new organizational culture.

Institutionalization features two different but related levels of learning. The first focuses on the individual. People adopt the new behavior because they can easily do it or because it yields some specific results. If a person also values those results, he or she is highly likely to adopt the desired behavior.

The second level of learning is at the level of the whole organization. Here, the learning of new behavior spreads from one or a few people to the behavior of the whole organization.

Three conditions must happen for learning to move from individuals to the entire organization. First, people must perceive others acting the new behavior. Second, they must share the belief that the new behavior is more right than the old. Third, they must believe that management will reward the new behavior. Those three conditions have clear implications for management actions to institutionalize a new organizational culture.

The physical setting of the organization must help social interaction and allow high visibility of others' behavior. Physical settings that do not let people see each other's behavior constrain institutionalization. The organization's communication system can overcome physical constraints. Nonprofit organizations with geographically dispersed locations, for example, can send information about the new organizational culture to all locations.

The degree of congruence between the new behavior and valued old behavior affects the shared belief that the new behavior is more right than the old. Cohesive groups and their norms play a role here. If those norms closely accord with the desired behavior, institutionalization happens fast. If they do not closely accord, the norms can act as a source of resistance to the change. Cohesive groups can strongly affect the adoption of behavior consistent with a new culture. Nonprofit organization managers should analyze the norms of cohesive groups in their organizations to see whether they accord with, or oppose, what is desired by the new culture.

The result of the institutionalization process is the persistence of the new behavior. An organization's socialization process and its reward system play key roles in reaching this result. The socialization process passes the new behaviors on to successive generations of employees. The reward system lets managers shape the behavior of newcomers and maintain the behavior of veterans. Both are major tools for institutionalizing a new culture in any organization.

27A.10   Conclusion

Organizational cultures include the values, norms, rites, rituals, symbols, ceremonies, heroes, and scoundrels in the history of the organization. Organizational cultures define what a new employee needs to learn for acceptance as a member of the organization. Cultural symbolism is a perspective on organizational culture that lets you view a culture as a system of symbols that have meaning only to members of that culture. Cultures are functional when they help an organization adapt to its external environment and coordinate internal activities. They are dysfunctional when they are the basis of resistance to change or create culture clashes when two different cultures merge.

The levels at which you see organizational cultures vary from visible to almost invisible. Artifacts and other cultural symbols usually are visible to even the newest employee. Basic assumptions, a set of implicit values, are almost invisible to new employees and are only learned after a period of socialization and acceptance. Espoused values and in-use values have midlevel visibility.

Diagnosing an organization's culture is an important way for a potential employee to get information about the organization. It also is an important way for a manager to learn about the culture of her organization. An outsider's diagnosis usually cannot go beyond artifacts and values. The insider not only sees artifacts and values but, with much work, can also uncover basic assumptions.

Managers maintain an existing organizational culture because they believe it is right for the environments they face. They also can try to change their culture to a new set of values, basic assumptions, and ideologies. Those new values can focus on diversity, quality, global competitiveness, or ethical behavior in the organization. Managers can try to create a new culture, usually in a separate work unit or in a new organization. The new culture needs a core ideology that is understandable, convincing, and widely discussed. Institutionalization is the process that sustains changes in an organization over time.

Suggested Readings

Alvesson, M., and P. O. Berg. (1992). *Corporate Culture and Organizational Symbolism*. Hawthorne, NY: Walter de Gruyter.

Argyris, C., and D. A. Schön. (1978). *Organizational Learning*. Reading, MA: Addison-Wesley.

Barney, J. B. (1986). "Organizational Culture: Can It Be a Source of Sustained Competitive Advantage?" *Academy of Management Review* 11:656–65.

Cameron, K. S. (1999). *Diagnosing and Changing Organizational Culture*. Reading, MA: Addison-Wesley Longman.

Cartwright, S., and C. L. Cooper. (1993). "The Role of Culture Compatibility in Successful Organizational Marriage." *Academy of Management Review* 7:57–70.

Champoux, J. E., and L. D. Goldman. (1993). "Building a Total Quality Culture." In T. D. Connors (ed.), *Nonprofit Organizations Policy and Procedures Handbook*. New York: John Wiley & Sons.

Dandridge, T. C., I. I. Mitroff, and W. F. Joyce. (1980). "Organizational Symbolism: A Topic to Expand Organizational Analysis," *Academy of Management Review* 5:77–82.

Deal, T. E., and A. A. Kennedy. (1982). *Corporate Cultures: The Rites and Rituals of Corporate Life*. Reading, MA: Addison-Wesley.

Denison, D., and A. Mishra. (1995). "Toward a Theory of Organizational Culture and Effectiveness," *Organization Science* 6:203–23.

Denison, D. R. (1990). *Corporate Culture and Organizational Effectiveness*. New York: John Wiley & Sons.

Drucker, P. F. (1990). *Managing the Non-Profit Organization*. New York: HarperCollins.

Gagliardi, P. (ed.). (1990). *Symbols and Artifacts: Views of the Corporate Landscape.* Hawthorne, NY: Walter de Gruyter.

Goodman, P. S., M. Bazerman, and E. Conlon. (1984). "Institutionalization of Planned Organizational Change." In B. M. Staw and L. L. Cummings (eds.), *Research in Organizational Behavior,* vol. 2. Greenwich, CT: JAI Press, pp. 215–46.

Kerr, J., and J. W. Slocum Jr. (1987). "Managing Corporate Culture through Reward Systems," *Academy of Management Executive* 1:99–108.

Levine, J. B. (1988). "Sun Microsystems Turns on the Afterburners," *Business Week* (July 18): 114–15, 118.

Loden, M., and J. B. Rosener. (1991). *Workforce America! Managing Employee Diversity as a Vital Resource.* Homewood, IL: Business One Irwin.

Martin, J. (1990). "Deconstructing Organizational Taboos: The Suppression of Gender Conflict in Organizations," *Organization Science* 1:339–59.

Martin, J. (1992). *Cultures in Organizations: Three Perspectives.* New York: Oxford University Press.

Nahavandi, A., and A. R. Malekzadeh. (1988). "Acculturation in Mergers and Acquisitions," *Academy of Management Review* 13:79–90.

Parker, M. (ed.). (2000). *Organizational Culture and Identity.* Thousand Oaks, CA: Sage Publications, Inc.

Pratt, M. G., and A. Rafaeli. (1997). "Organizational Dress as a Symbol of Multilayered Social Identities," *Academy of Management Journal* 40:862–98.

Schein, E. H. (1984). "Coming to a New Awareness of Organizational Culture," *Sloan Management Review* 25:3–16.

Schein, E. H. (1992). *Organizational Culture and Leadership.* San Francisco: Jossey-Bass.

Trice, H. M., and J. M. Beyer. (1993). *The Cultures of Work Organizations.* Englewood Cliffs, NJ: Prentice Hall.

Van Maanen, J., and G. Kunda. (1989). "Real Feelings: Emotional Expression and Organizational Culture." In B. M. Staw and L. L. Cummings (eds.), *Research in Organizational Behavior,* vol 2. Greenwich, CT: JAI Press, pp. 43–103.

Verity, J. M. (1992). "Does IBM Get It Now?" *Business Week* (December 28): 32–33.

Walter, G. (1985). "Culture Collisions in Mergers and Acquisitions." In P. Frost, L. Moore, M. Louis, C. Lundberg, and J. Martin (eds.), *Organizational Culture.* Beverly Hills, CA: Sage Publications, pp. 301–314.

Watkins, A. L., and N. J. Bristow. (1987). "For Successful Organizational Culture, Honor Your Past," *Academy of Management Executive* 1:221–29.

Wilkins, A. L., and W. G. Ouchi. (1983). "Efficient Cultures: Exploring the Relationship between Culture and Organizational Performance," *Administrative Science Quarterly* 28:468–81.

Endnotes

1. From *Organizational Behavior: Essential Tenets for a New Millennium, 1st edition,* by J. E. Champoux. © 2000. Reprinted with permission of South-Western College Publishing, a division of Thomson Learning. Fax (800) 730-2215 and from *Organizational Behavior: Integrating Individuals, Groups, and Processes, 1st edition,* by J. E. Champoux. © 1996. Reprinted with permission

of South-Western College Publishing, a division of Thomson Learning. Fax (800) 730-2215.

2. Argyris and Schön use the concept of "theory in use." I use a slightly modified label for the concept to allow parallel structure in this context.

3. Martin, J. (1990). "Deconstructing Organizational Taboos: The Suppression of Gender Conflict in Organizations," *Organization Science* 1:339–59.

4. A different version of this section appeared in J. E. Champoux and L. B. Goldman. (1993). "Building a Total Quality Culture." In T. D. Connors (ed.), *The Nonprofit Management Handbook: Operating Policies and Procedures.* New York: John Wiley & Sons, Inc., pp. 64–65.

Volunteer Organization Management Processes and Challenges in the International Context (New)

DONNA KENNEDY-GLANS, BA, LLB
The Kennedy-Glans Perspective Inc.

34A.1 Context and Introduction

In our increasingly interconnected world, markets, nations, and technologies are integrated to a degree never before experienced. Enhanced communication mechanisms, including online methodologies, have fostered the exchange of ideas, information, and strategies among and between members of local, national, and transnational volunteer organizations. Channels of communication and influence between volunteer organizations and private- and public-sector groups are also stronger. Best practices can be shared on a worldwide basis, and issues and their resolution are now contemplated within a global and integrated context. Nonprofit/nongovernment organizations are consequently encouraged to reexamine their mandates, in particular, the geographical boundaries of their spheres of influence.

Traditional, rational, and even international boundaries between politics, culture, technology, finance, national security, and ecology are disappearing. Destabilization means shifting contexts, leaving both public and private sectors struggling with how to develop strategies and mechanisms which are socially accountable and flexible, yet capable of delivering value on many levels. In responding to the enormity of the challenges, alignment of the objectives of all stakeholders, including the nonprofit sector, is critical to success—piece-meal or isolated initiatives are not nearly as effective or sustainable. The role of the voluntary organization in the development and implementation of strategies that respond to these complex global challenges is becoming more important and credible.

When evaluating nonprofit mandates within a globalized context, volunteer organizations are encouraged to apply management processes that have the ability to objectively gauge the consequences of extending objectives beyond North American boundaries. The local and international reputation and potential of a voluntary organization will be impacted, positively or negatively, by how it manages its risks and challenges in an international setting. Nonprofit organizations are encouraged to assess their organizational capacity to participate in international initiatives, and their ability to respond effectively to risks that may be encountered within this expanded mandate.

34A.2 *Framework for Analysis of Management Processes to Minimize Risk in International Operations and Maximize Reputation and Organizational Potential*

For the purpose of examining key management issues and challenges facing volunteer organizations evaluating or pursuing international opportunities, two case studies will be discussed.

The first case study describes the experiences of a Canadian-based volunteer medical team that has been successful in recruiting experienced medical doctors and specialists to assist in reducing infant and maternal mortality rates in Yemen. The highly qualified medical team has been providing ongoing capacity building support within the Yemeni medical system for over a decade. Although this volunteer medical team has enjoyed enormous success, they find themselves asking questions as they reexamine their role and objectives, and their future direction.

The second case showcases a volunteer team at a different stage in its development. A U.S.-based volunteer legal organization is considering expansion of its mandate to include international objectives. The legal aid organization is successful in its local mandate, but is enticed by the invitation to provide human rights legal support and training to lawyers in Nigeria. This volunteer team is student based, and membership evolves as students cycle through the local law school.

Examining these two cases allows you, the practitioner, to step inside the decision-making processes that management faces within volunteer organizations when mandates and objectives are being established, or reexamined, in an international context. Key issues are presented in these case studies, and processes and strategies for evaluation and management of international risks and opportunities are assessed. Whether you are managing within an organization actively engaged in international opportunities, or advising a volunteer team that is considering extension of the geographical boundaries of its mandate and influence, the case studies and the management processes discussed should be useful.

(A) CASE 1: MEDICAL OUTREACH TEAM IN YEMEN

The Team. A team of highly experienced Canadian medical doctors and specialists, working under the volunteer leadership of a very committed individual, has been traveling to Yemen once or twice a year for the last 13 years. Bonds of friendship and respect among members of this volunteer team are strong. The team is comprised of a core of retired and quasi-retired professionals, and is supplemented by other practitioners on an ad-hoc basis.

The team very effectively manages cultural issues, and is sensitive in their approach to the Yemeni at all government and operational levels. Establishing trust with Yemeni government officials and with sectoral counterparts has been a priority. Leaders within the Yemeni government, and practitioners in Yemen's health and education sectors, are openly appreciative of the volunteer team's nonthreatening, apolitical, and supportive approach. Managing corruption in a discreet and appropriate manner is capably handled by the team. Security risks are closely monitored and thoughtfully evaluated in planning and implementing missions.

The Objectives. The volunteer team's laudable goal is to assist in the reduction of infant and maternal mortality in Yemen. By sharing best practices with local Yemeni doctors, health care administrators, local communities, and the Ministries of Health and Higher Education, this medical team is able to create templates of expertise for the Yemeni in their management of infant and maternal mortality. The strategy utilized by the volunteer team to achieve this objective is to focus on the teaching of medical faculty at senior university or hospital levels. By emphasizing this *teach the teachers* model, the volunteer team is able to leverage the advantage of the best practices sharing as widely as possible, and enhance sustainability.

The objectives of the medical team are determined on the basis of Yemeni priorities, and are not imposed based on western assessments of need. Within their medical system, Yemen governmental and medical organizations have identified infant and maternal mortality as a high priority. World Bank and other multilateral research affirm these assessments.

The Stakeholders. Given that management of health care in Yemen is strongly influenced by the Yemeni government, the volunteer team focuses on relationships within the medical and governmental communities. Relationships with multinational and local corporations operating in Yemen are also mutually advantageous. As well, frequent and open collaboration with World Bank and other donor organizations in Yemen has maximized the potential for integrated efforts to achieve reductions in infant and maternal mortality rates.

(B) CASE 2: LAW STUDENT VOLUNTEERS

The Team. Under the mentorship of designated law professors within a U.S. law school, teams of volunteer law students provide pro bono legal advice to lower income families through a volunteer association founded within the law school umbrella. Several of the professorial mentors are very dedicated, and use these situations to coach and teach the students about legal issues and relationships with clients. Although part of their teaching duties, some mentors apply exceptional energy to ensure the effectiveness of this program.

The volunteer law students are generally in their final year of formal studies, and are interested in securing hands-on experience, and in responding to local community needs. Although some second-year students participate in the legal aid program, the core of the volunteer team generally turns over on an annual basis as the students graduate.

The Objectives. There are several objectives to the legal aid program. By contributing free legal advice to lower income families, the program is intended to enhance access to legal advice within the local community. Typical legal issues include rent reviews, simple contract analysis, insolvency, matrimonial matters, and small claims court applications. In fulfilling this mandate, the law school achieves the objective of enhancing its reputation within that same community. Also, the program underscores with students—the future lawyers—the importance and value of their social accountabilities as professionals. Finally, the experiences avail students the opportunity to relate to clients and address issues within a legal framework in advance of graduation; students can hone their skills and confirm their areas of interest.

These nonprofit objectives are determined by the legal aid society within the administrative structure of the law school. The professional mentors greatly influence the means to realize the objectives (establishing procedures and standards), but the entire law school faculty and university management oversee the scope of this volunteer initiative. The students are not actively involved in determining the objectives.

The Stakeholders. Direct beneficiaries of this volunteer program include members of the local community who access the free legal advice, and the students who gain experience through their volunteer work. The law school and the university are important stakeholders in the program, and their reputation is directly impacted by the program's success or failure. The dedicated mentors are assigned to the organization and administration of these volunteer activities, and their level of support and interest depends on their individual approach to the social value of the volunteer work. The local law society is very involved in ensuring that standards of professionalism are maintained. The local government is engaged to ensure that *needs* assessments are consistent with other standards within their jurisdiction.

34A.3 *Reevaluation of Mandates and Objectives by Volunteer Organizations: The Catalyst*

The catalyst for a volunteer organization to reexamine its mandate and objectives may be either internal or external. In the two scenarios described above, each volunteer organization has encountered challenges, or opportunities, that encourage the members and their sponsors to pause and reevaluate their direction. In the case of the volunteer medical team, internal questions about the sustainability of their effectiveness are the trigger. In the case of the volunteer legal aid team, the externally initiated opportunity to apply their volunteer efforts in an international context motivates the organization to reassess its mandate. Regardless of the "trigger" for the evaluation process, volunteer organizations operating, or seeking to operate, within an international context must ask themselves some key questions, and must develop strategies on the basis of their honest responses to these queries.

The volunteer Canadian medical team traveling to Yemen recognizes that the key challenge to the *sustainability* of its mandate is the ongoing recruitment of experienced volunteer doctors and specialists to participate in the missions, particularly in the context of shortages of medical expertise in North America. Work schedules for medical practitioners are often inflexible, making sporadic participation in international missions difficult to coordinate. Attracting younger doctors is somewhat impacted by the inability of the nonprofit organization to provide an adequate level of financial support for volunteers. In response to this constraint, the nonprofit organization has taken the time to reevaluate its overall mandate, objectives, and strategies for achieving and measuring these outcomes.

The American legal aid group is prompted to reexamine the scope of its mandate in response to an external opportunity. One of the professional mentors who has been involved in management of the legal aid program for several years is dedicated to the global advancement of human rights, and an opportunity arises as a result of her recognized expertise. Specifically, a recently elected Nigerian Senator, under the leadership of democratically elected President Obasanjo, has inquired as to the feasibility of this U.S. professor facilitating the training of Nigerian lawyers in the field of human rights. The suggestion is made that American law students with recognized ability in this area of practice be sent to Nigeria to work closely with Nigerian legal practitioners, thereby facilitating an exchange of best practices and legal precedents for respecting human rights. The human rights professor, and several of her senior students, are excited by this opportunity and organize meetings within the legal aid group to discuss the feasibility of expanding the geographical horizon and scope of the nonprofit legal organization to incorporate this global human rights initiative.

34A.4 Management Processes and Strategies to Identify and Manage Risks and Challenges in an International Context

Risks and opportunities must be carefully assessed and measured in any context, but participation by a nonprofit organization in an international context adds more complexity to the analysis and strategies. To ensure that your nonprofit organization considers all the steps in identifying and analyzing risks, and in developing and implementing responsive strategies, a process for risk evaluation and response is represented in Exhibit 34A.1.

This process advocated for risk assessment and management in international initiatives is broad based and integrative. The analysis of risks is an important first step in the process, but the true "value add" for a volunteer organization comes with the incorporation of this analysis into strategies that respond to an organization's

EXHIBIT 34A.1   Risk Evaluation and Response

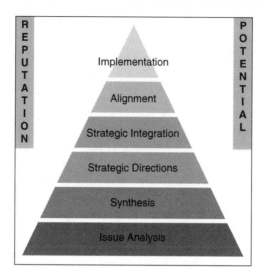

EXHIBIT 34A.2   Risk Assessment and Management Processes

unique opportunities, capacities, and direction. The process encourages your management and operational decision makers to tailor and implement strategies that are practical, responsive to the unique risks of a given situation, and maximize an organization's potential and reputation.

To illustrate how the process in this pyramid operates in assessing and managing risk in an international context, this chapter will review the key issues of the volunteer teams in the two case studies. Their respective issues are identified below (see Exhibit 34A.2), and subsequent discussion will track the organization's evaluation and ultimate management of the issues and risks through the process pyramid.

34A.5   Risk Assessment and Management Processes

(A) PUBLIC IMAGE AND REPUTATION

A nonprofit organization's public image and reputation in its local environment will be impacted, positively or negatively, by its international pursuits. In an increasingly global world, you must assume that no organizational action is immune from public scrutiny. Volunteer organizations must ensure that all decisions made, domestically and internationally, achieve the objective of preserving the organization's reputation.

In the case of the volunteer medical team operating in Yemen, their reputation in Yemen and Canada is preserved through apolitical capacity building support to the Yemeni medical and health education systems. Careful screening of the volunteers attempts to identify religious, economic, or other motivators that could complicate a political operation. For example, a volunteer actively advocating Christian beliefs and values in Yemen, a predominantly Islamic country, could potentially compromise the reputation of the entire volunteer team, and the team's effectiveness.

On occasion, the volunteer medical team has been invited to provide independent assessments of medical conditions and capacity building strategies in other developing countries in the Middle East. In determining whether to participate in medical evaluations of infant and maternal care strategies in jurisdictions where local leadership has been sanctioned or condemned by the western world, the volunteer team had openly discussed their participation from the perspective of their worldwide reputation. When the team has elected to proceed with the medical evaluation, this decision has been made on the clear understanding that their participation in the host country is an apolitical act that in no way condemns or condones the actions of the host government. A firm stance on their apolitical role is important as local politicians and foreign investors have on occasion attempted to draw the delegation into the political fray.

In the case of the volunteer legal aid organization, its current reputation and public image are largely relevant within the local community only. Beneficiaries of the legal aid work, stakeholders within the university and the law school, the governing law society, and the local community pay close attention to the organization's reputation. However, if the organization decides to expand its mandate to include the provision of human rights support and training to Nigerian lawyers, the public image and reputation of the volunteer organization will grow exponentially. By revising the nature and geographical range of its activities, the organization is opening up its reputation to scrutiny by international human rights experts and associations, supporters and critics of Nigeria's recent democratization, the Nigerian legal profession, Nigerian society in general, and a multitude of other impacted parties. In order to measure up in these assessments, the law school must ensure that it has the capacity to provide the necessary human rights training and support.

If the legal aid association elects to create a dual mandate, a stellar reputation in exercise of its domestic mandate will not preserve its reputation internationally. Similarly, blights on the organization's reputation or public image resulting from its international operations could compromise the group's domestic image.

In the case of a volunteer organization with very divergent mandates, the public may be confused by the images presented. With its current objectives, the legal aid society is perceived by the local community as a synergistic combination of the university's desire to offer hands-on experience to rookie lawyers, and the extension of charitable support to low-income families in need of legal advice. The addition of a mandate to train Nigerian lawyers in human rights law offers a radically different public image of the volunteer organization as an international development support agency focused on alleviating human rights abuses in the developing world. Both mandates are laudable in terms of public benefit, but the image of the volunteer organization may become confusing to the public.

(B) POLITICAL/SOCIAL/ECONOMIC ENVIRONMENT

Notwithstanding the intention of a volunteer organization to provide apolitical support in a developing country, the organization must closely examine the political, social, and economic context of the host jurisdiction to maximize effectiveness and manage risk. Delivery of volunteer services must be tailored in each community to ensure that cultural norms are respected. Volunteers must recognize and accommodate the unique political, social, and economic constraints, or opportunities, within the host culture. Cultural sensitivity training may be a prerequisite for volunteer engagement with representatives of the host jurisdiction.

In the early stages of participation in Yemen, the medical volunteers in our case study relied on the expertise of members of the team with experience in Saudi Arabia. The team's success is attributable to their appreciation that religious and local spiritual practices and values have to be respected. Living and health conditions in Yemen, both in general and as they specifically affect maternal and infant health, are carefully considered. Values and expectations about health, and the impact of high infant and maternal mortality, are understood in a Yemeni context. Approaches to patient care, in particular the treatment of females, are carefully considered to minimize the risk of unintentional offence. The participation of women volunteers on the team is addressed—the Yemeni welcome female doctors, but the issue is first identified and evaluated.

Yemen is a relatively poor country, and many of the supports to medical care that we take for granted in western jurisdictions cannot be assumed. For example, although refrigeration may be available to store blood and other medical supplies requiring refrigeration, generators to power the refrigerators are not always accessible, thereby compromising the capacity of local medical care. Strategies developed to support Yemen in its reduction of maternal and infant mortality rates are successful because they acknowledge and anticipate these unique cultural, political, social, and economic conditions.

In the case of the legal aid organization contemplating a human rights training project in Nigeria, the team must appreciate that democracy in Nigeria is in its infancy. Democratization is a journey, not a destination, and it will take time for Nigeria to reform all of its social, political, and economic institutions to respect democratic principles of transparency and broad citizen participation in decision making. The role of a militia in a civilian government is still being resolved. Citizens' expectations for change in human rights enforcement by the Nigerian judicial system, the police, and the military may not be realistic, and public frustration should be anticipated. These complex socioeconomic impacts of democratization must be understood and respected by the volunteer teams.

Human rights abuses by the Nigerian military were notorious under General Abacha's former military dictatorship. Volunteers must be aware of the pervasiveness of these abuses, and the hurdles to reform that still exist. In North America, lawyers have precedents and legislation to assist in the definition and legal response to discriminatory employment practices, or use of excessive force by police officers. Nigeria's legal system does not share the same capacity to enforce human rights legislation and values, even under the new democratic leadership of President Obasanjo.

In order to understand the catalysts for human rights abuses in Nigeria, and potential solutions, volunteers must take time to research and analyze the basis for racial and religious tensions among sectors of the Nigerian population. Clashes between tribes, and between Islamic and Christian adherents, historically triggered abuses by Nigerian police and militia. Economic disparities between the poor but oil-rich Christians in southern Nigeria, and the Islamic seat of political and economic power in northern Nigeria, exacerbate the racial and religious conflicts. The enactment of human rights legislation is not a panacea that will resolve these deeply rooted tensions.

Assessments and analysis of political, social, and economic conditions in a host jurisdiction must also be evaluated in a regional context. For example, although Nigeria is a sovereign state that enacts its own human rights legislation and appoints its own judiciary and police to uphold these laws, human rights compliance in Nigeria should also be considered in the context of West Africa. If few of Nigeria's geographical neighbors value human rights compliance, it will be challenging for Nigeria to impose and enforce its higher standards in relation to Nigerian militia deployed to peacekeeping missions in Sierre Leone and elsewhere in the region.

(C) SECURITY AND SAFETY

Ensuring the safety and security of individuals representing your volunteer organization in host jurisdictions is a critical priority. Apolitical volunteers have historically been considered immune to most security risks. However, the recent murders of Red Cross workers in Sudan, Nigeria, and Colombia underscore the shortcomings of such assumptions.

In the case of Yemen, threats by religious extremists periodically escalate security risks. Tribal challenges to authority are sometimes expressed through kidnappings of foreigners, and although generally nonviolent, the kidnapping of a volunteer by a Yemeni tribe would attract media attention.

Nigeria's democratic evolution has heightened expectations for reform, and violence has escalated. Volunteers supporting human rights training in Nigeria may be innocent victims of local violence or criminal activity. The risk of violence varies throughout the country, and the level of risk in each local community must be evaluated independently.

In addition to security risks in the international jurisdiction, volunteer organizations must assess the medical and physical safety of their members. What diseases are prevalent, and what inoculations are recommended or required? Notwithstanding local norms, should volunteers be required to wear seat belts in vehicles? Are there other safety risks that need to be addressed in the particular jurisdiction?

Potential liability to the volunteer organization is a significant consideration in an international operation. Safety and security issues must be clearly analyzed and disclosed to members of your volunteer organization. Allocation and apportionment of potential responsibility for breaches of security and safety must be determined in advance of a crisis. How will any potential kidnappings be handled? Who is liable if a volunteer contracts a life-threatening virus? What level of security protection will be guaranteed by the volunteer organization? What will be the consequence of a volunteer's disregard for recommended risk precautions?

(D) ETHICS AND GOVERNANCE

The provision of volunteer support in a developing country may expose volunteers to corrupt business practices. Every host jurisdiction is unique, and nonprofit organizations must do their homework in assessing the risk of bribes and kickbacks being regarded as generally accepted business practices in an international project. Volunteer organizations have a legal and ethical responsibility to develop strategies to manage these risks.

Foreign corrupt practices are defined and made illegal by applicable American and Canadian legislation, and by Organization for Economic Cooperation and Development (OECD) and other multilateral guidelines. It is recommended that nonprofit organizations operating in jurisdictions recognized for their corrupt business practices talk to their legal advisers about specific legal constraints. Volunteers participating in these jurisdictions should also be provided with support by the organization in handling situations where bribes are being paid, or where dubious business practices are in operation. Dealings with agents and local partners need particular scrutiny. If corruption is a significant issue in the host jurisdiction, the nonprofit organization should consider the creation of an express statement of values for the organization, and discuss and generate guidelines for your volunteers when operating in the host jurisdiction.

Transparency International and other international agencies have assessed that both Yemen and Nigeria are countries where corruption is a risk. The Canadian medical doctors operating in Yemen are low-key about the issue of potential corruption in Yemen, but are cautious to ensure that their activities are not viewed as supporting any such practices. In Nigeria, corruption is a major issue; one of the top priorities of the new democratic leadership is to develop best practices for management of this issue, across sectors. It is likely that the Nigerian partners in a human rights project will have guidelines for corruption management that can be considered by the volunteer American legal aid team.

(E) SOCIAL ACCOUNTABILITIES

Engagement in international jurisdictions, particularly in the developing world, will undoubtedly raise the issue of social accountability for the nonprofit organization. How can a western volunteer team provide support to a beneficiary in the developing world in a way that is sustainable? Does the strategy deployed to provide this volunteer support involve any express or implicit imposition of western values? What is the likely socioeconomic impact of the volunteer support in the host country? How can host jurisdiction expectations of donor impact be appropriately managed to militate against disappointment and frustration?

These questions about social accountability are very complex and challenging, but they must be asked in order for nonprofit organizations to identify not only *what* projects to participate in, but also *how* to participate. Third-party assessments of sustainability and socioeconomic impact of donor support may be desirable to ensure objectivity.

The Canadian medical team offering support to Yemen attributes its ongoing effectiveness to a careful consideration of its social accountabilities in Yemen. Offering episodical support to Yemen's medical and health education systems is not their preferred approach; a more effective methodology would be to have constant support for the Yemeni provided by in-country medical experts from Canada. However, the only option financially and logistically available to the volunteer team is to build relationships of trust with key health experts and teachers in Yemen, and to offer focused capacity building support to key Yemenis through volunteer missions, supplemented by long-distance support on an ongoing basis. Coordination with other stakeholder strategies in Yemen is a critical consideration in the establishment of a sustainable strategy that can offer continuity of presence to the Yemeni medical and health education systems. Further, the medical team has been very careful to only promise the Yemeni what they can deliver—expectations are managed and trust is sustained.

It will be critical for the volunteer legal aid association to incorporate social accountability considerations into its analysis of a proposed expansion of their nonprofit mandate to include human rights issues in Nigeria. Human rights education, training, and enforcement in Nigeria are overwhelming goals that will require the participation and support of thousands of organizations within and beyond Nigeria. The objectives are laudable, but the task is daunting. Although human rights are an internationally recognized entitlement of all people, respect for human rights in a Nigerian context requires enormous support to achieve theoretical and practical implementation. The nonprofit legal organization must closely examine how its contribution to this enormous initiative will support sustainable advancement of these objectives in Nigeria. Will sporadic exchanges of best practices be sufficient to raise the level of understanding, awareness, and knowledge in the Nigerian legal community, or is it preferable for the volunteer legal organization to align with a larger international nonprofit entity or entities in a must sustainable effort?

Finally, the legal aid association must ask itself if the goal of advancing the human rights knowledge base and experience of its own volunteers is an important priority of participation in this Nigerian initiative. If education of the volunteers is a priority objective, the nonprofit organization must consider the extent to which this educational objective supports or hinders the sharing of best practices for human rights compliance in Nigeria.

(F) STAKEHOLDER ENGAGEMENT

The identification of stakeholders is a critical first step in recognizing risks and determining strategies for nonprofit organizations in international projects. Globalization has expanded geographical and sectoral stakeholder horizons. Not only will other volunteer organizations, within North America and internationally, be interested in the outcomes of your engagement in a host country, but local and international governmental and private-sector players, and perhaps the media, will be paying attention as well.

EXHIBIT 34A.3 Stakeholder Group

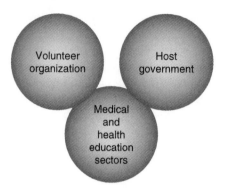

A stakeholder is widely defined by academics as *any group or individual who can affect or is affected by the achievement of the organization's objectives.* On the basis of this comprehensive definition, stakeholders of a volunteer organization are not limited to the volunteers, the donors, and the beneficiaries. Rather, nonprofit organizations must acknowledge the objectives and priorities of many groups and individuals, including local, national, and international volunteer or advocacy organizations; corporations with interests in the affected jurisdictions; governmental institutions in North America and in the host jurisdiction; local communities in the host jurisdiction; the World Bank, the World Health Organization, the International Monetary Fund, and other multilateral organizations; and the local and international media.

The Canadian medical team supporting Yemen's improvement in maternal and infant mortality statistics recognizes the importance of their stakeholder group, and alliances. In Yemen, the volunteer team recognizes its key partnership with the Yemeni medical and health education sectors, and Yemeni government representatives at very senior and strategic levels, as illustrated in Exhibit 34A.3.

The volunteer team also understands that its objectives affect, or are affected by, the objectives of the following additional players: representatives of Yemeni civil society, the diplomatic core, the local media, local and international private-sector investors, and representatives of multilateral and nonprofit organizations focused on health care delivery and support in Yemen, as illustrated in Exhibit 34A.4.

Outside Yemen, the medical team has prioritized relationships and rationalized strategies with Canadian governmental representatives, the Yemeni and Middle Eastern diplomatic core, health education institutes including local universities, multilateral institutions engaged in health care support to Yemen and other developing countries, donors who support the voluntary organization's initiatives, the medical profession, private-sector investors in Yemen and the Middle East, and the media.

The volunteer medical team's recognition of an expansive stakeholder group, and its collaborative approach to stakeholders, has been a cornerstone of its success in Yemen. By aligning and coordinating strategies with international and local Yemeni health care organizations, the medical team has enhanced the impact of

EXHIBIT 34A.4   Additional Players

its volunteer services. Synergistic strategies among donors have been important as the objective of reducing maternal and infant mortality rates in Yemen is complex and requires a multipronged and integrated medical and health education approach to achieve success.

Likewise, the team's recognition of the role of the Yemeni government in setting priorities for Yemen health, and in designating priorities for limited financial and nonfinancial resources within Yemen, has proven prudent. Ensuring that their objectives are consistent with the priorities of the Yemeni government enables the medical team to advance implementation of its best practices sharing program in an effective and strategic manner. Local health care providers recognize that their own government is supportive, and this State endorsement expedites the absorption of the training benefits and encourages local participants to deliver on their commitments.

Alliances with Canadian and North American stakeholders enable the Canadian medical team to access medical expertise from a broader base. These relationships also facilitate a strengthening of Canadian–Yemeni diplomatic relations, recently culminating in a multiparty approach to the Canadian International Development Agency to facilitate longer-term support by Canada to Yemen's medical needs.

In the wake of growing private-sector responsiveness to social accountabilities in development projects, the medical team is encouraged by the interest and support for their volunteer work emanating from local and international corporate investors in Yemen. A well-respected Yemeni company is instrumental in providing infrastructure and financial support to the volunteer doctors in a region of Yemen where the company is operating. Likewise, a large Canadian investor in

Yemen's energy sector is responsive to the volunteer team's needs for financial and logistic support. These corporations recognize the value to all stakeholders of enhanced longer-term relationships between Yemen and Canada, and their interest in these relationships extends beyond the commercial confines of an individual project or transaction. This private-sector support for the medical initiative also garners the companies' recognition in the local communities where they operate, and the respect of Yemeni leadership. *Chequebook charity* is no longer the predictable norm in corporate philanthropy—the private sector is seeking active engagement with nonprofit organizations and the larger communities in which they operate.

When assessing its stakeholder group and potential synergies, the legal aid association must think broadly and comprehensively. There are many local and international groups and individuals affected by human rights training in Nigeria, and which can affect this training. Alliances with international human rights advocacy groups should be encouraged to ensure an alignment of objectives and implementation strategies. Local North American stakeholders are also critical— interested parties represent a valuable resource from which financial, logistical, and professional support can potentially be drawn. Stakeholders within Nigeria must also be recognized, and their expectations and needs must be addressed in developing and implementing strategies. The media can be a useful ally in achieving human rights education and respect in Nigeria, but they will also focus international attention on any foibles or flaws. The volunteer group must recognize that private-sector investors are affected by human rights training and compliance; corresponding impacts on their relationships and operations in Nigeria, and their global reputations, should be considered.

(G) ORGANIZATIONAL CAPACITY

In assessing the risks and threats to conducting volunteer activities in an international context, your nonprofit organization must candidly and honestly assess its organizational capacity. Is your organization equipped to effectively manage identified and anticipated risks in the international context? Every organization has unique capabilities and strengths, and you must assess whether your organization's capacities are aligned with the international mandate being evaluated or reviewed. The task of assessing organizational capacity is challenging in any context, but may become a particularly thorny issue with a group of well-intended and highly motivated volunteers.

If you judge that your organizational capacity is deficient, there are measures that can be taken to supplement your team's ability to manage the international context under consideration. Expertise from other nonprofit organizations may be a valuable source of intelligence and experience. As an interim measure, it may be preferable for your volunteer team to reside under the umbrella of a more experienced nonprofit organization until your team's capacity is sufficiently bolstered. Do not hesitate to look beyond the nonprofit sector for support—private-sector and governmental experience in a host jurisdiction may be accessible and practical.

When a nonprofit organization evaluates the viability of expanding the geographical boundaries of its present mandate, it is likely that the organizational capacity of the group to achieve its *current* mandate will be well developed and recognized for excellence. However, responding effectively to an international mandate may require additional or different skill sets and expertise. In order to position your organization for transition into an international context, you must determine your organizational needs in the new environment, and motivate your volunteers to confirm that these capacities are met before stepping forward to pursue the international opportunity.

In reexamining organizational capacity, the volunteer medical team was frank in acknowledging that constraints in attracting younger doctors to participate was a potential hurdle to maintaining a desired level of support to Yemen. In response to this identified need, the group examined several options, including alignment with other multilateral organizations and nonprofit initiatives. One option that is presently being pursued as a means of securing financial and operational stability in the longer term is a request for developmental support and funding from the Canadian International Development Agency. A submission to the Canadian development agency has implications for the volunteer team, as it will necessarily involve the active participation of Canadian governmental and educational institutions, thereby diminishing some of the team's independence. However, if approved, the sponsorship should foster a strengthening of diplomatic ties between Canada and Yemen, and will sustain the positive measures that have been initiated by the volunteer medical team in relation to reducing infant and maternal mortality rates in Yemen.

Organizational capacity for the volunteer legal team is a significant challenge. The skills and capabilities required to facilitate the provision of free legal advice in the local community are enormously different from the capacity required to support Nigeria in its human rights training and education objectives. The law school professor with human rights expertise clearly has the talents and qualifications to provide human rights training to Nigerian lawyers, but the ability of law students to provide such support on an effective and sustainable basis is questionable. Although capacity building within the existing legal aid structure is viable, it is unclear whether this focus on human rights is appealing to the volunteers required to support such a program. Also, diverting financial and logistical support from the existing legal aid program will negatively impact the local community and other local stakeholders who support the existing mandate.

An invitation by a Nigerian Senator to participate in human rights training in a new democracy is exciting. However, this international mandate is difficult to reconcile with the existing local mandate of the nonprofit organization. The organizational capacity requirements are very different, and the respective local and international mandates have little in common. As an interim measure, it is ultimately determined that the human rights expert within the law school will be encouraged to participate in the human rights training initiative in Nigeria, and may hand-select capable and motivated students to assist in this project. However, this voluntary initiative will not be conducted under the auspices of the U.S.-based legal aid society. Rather, the professor and selected students will provide volunteer support through an internationally recognized human rights organization that is presently active in Nigeria. The law school is confident in the capacity of the professor to contribute effectively to the human rights training goals in Nigeria, and the law school's local and international reputation will be enhanced by this international volunteer activity of its staff and students.

34A.6 Conclusion

Nonprofit organizations are both exhilarated and daunted by the challenge of reevaluating their mandates within an international context. Organizations will quickly realize that cookie-cutter approaches to this evaluation process will not be effective—volunteer organizations have unique capabilities and mandates, and homogenization of nonprofit initiatives is not the goal of globalization.

The question for strategic leaders within nonprofit organizations has evolved from an identification of *what* projects to participate in to *how* voluntary initiatives should be determined and implemented. As a consequence of globalization, many local initiatives can now be seen through a geographically expanded lens. Volunteer organizations must assess the most effective means to achieve their organization's mandate—should the initiative maintain its local context, or will achievement of the organization's objectives be significantly embellished through international synergy and engagement?

The value of cooperation with like-minded stakeholders is becoming increasingly evident in nonprofit alliances—organizations are asking, "What can best be done together that cannot be done individually?" Some objectives are more clearly achievable in cooperation with others. In the cases reviewed, both organizations had a professional context that is very relevant. The volunteer medical team recognizes the enormous medical fraternity that exists worldwide, and has tapped into this wealth of experience and expertise to support their initiative. However, the "connector" among stakeholders is not limited to professional attributes—the shared values and goals can be derived from many sources.

Expanding your organization's geographical horizons can be an excellent means to invigorate your volunteer team's mandate, can be very rewarding to volunteers, and can achieve measurable success in responding to true need. However, the decision to step into the international arena should not be taken casually. As decisions about international mandates are evaluated, decision makers within nonprofit organizations are encouraged to adopt systems and processes that promote the identification and management of key issues and risks. Internal and external expectations of geographically expanded mandates must be addressed. Impacts to your organization's reputation and potential must be assessed. Once embarked on the international pathway, you must keep checking your assessments about risks and opportunities, and challenge the effectiveness of your strategies to respond to the identified threats. Circumstances can change in host jurisdictions, and your organization's strategies must be flexible enough to respond to shifts in risks and opportunities.

The most significant source of information for this paper originates from the author's experiences working with nongovernmental organizations and private-sector partnerships worldwide. In particular, alliances with Transparency International and Nigerian-based advocacy organizations in their individual and collective efforts to address corruption in Nigeria were useful in illustrating the issues to be addressed by the volunteer legal aid organization. The author's experiences in supporting the humanitarian initiatives of a Canadian medical team in Yemen, as well as private-sector experience in the Middle East, provided insights into the risks to be evaluated by the Canadian medical team, and the effectiveness of strategies implemented. The author is enormously grateful to the Canadian medical team for their exemplary example of how to provide capacity building support in the developing world, and for their support and advice in preparing this paper.

Suggested Readings

Bray, J. (1999). "Petroleum and Human Rights: The New Frontiers of Debate," *Oil and Gas Journal* 97(44): 65–69.

Friedman, T. (2000). *The Lexus and the Olive Tree.* New York: Anchor Books.

Gharajedaghi, J. (1999). *Systems Thinking: Managing Chaos and Complexity—A Platform for Designing Business Architecture.* Boston: Butterworth-Heinemann.

Inter-Church Action for Development, Relief and Justice, *Inter-Church Action Annual Report 1999/2000, www.web.ca/~icact.*

McPhail, K., and A. Davy. (1998). *Integrating Social Concerns into Private Sector Decision Making: A Review of Corporate Practices in the Mining, Oil and Gas Sectors.* World Bank, Washington, DC.

Schwartz, P., and B. Gibb. (1999). *When Good Companies Do Bad Things: Responsibility and Risk in an Age of Globalization.* New York: John Wiley & Sons, Inc.

Index